Piddinghoe Church

THE OLD

PARISH CHURCHES

OF SUSSEX

Mike Salter

FOLLY PUBLICATIONS

ACKNOWLEDGEMENTS

The photographs and plans in this book are the product of fieldwork by the author between 1979 and 1999. The author also drew the maps and sketches. The old prints, postcards and brass rubbings are reproduced from originals in his collection. The author would like to thank Sara-Sue Lovatt and Kerin Fogarty for assistance with transport and accommodation during the fieldwork for this book.

ABOUT THIS BOOK

As with the other church books in this series (see full list inside back cover) this book concentrates on the period before the Industrial Revolution of the late 18th century and the development of seaside resorts necessitated the construction of a fresh series of churches to serve the new urban areas. Most furnishings and monuments after 1800 are not mentioned, although additions and alterations to older churches usually are. Churches founded after 1800 are not mentioned in the gazetteers, nor do they appear on the maps, but they are listed with some brief details in separate sections.

Unlike some of the other books in the series, this volume uses the modern boundaries. The boundary between East Sussex and West Sussex was substantially altered in 1974. Readers will find that about twenty churches listed in this book as being in West Sussex appear in older books and maps as being in East Sussex.

This book is inevitably very much a catalogue of descriptions, date and names. It is intended as a field guide and for reference rather than to be read from cover to cover. Occasionally there are comments about the settings of churches but on the whole lack of space permits few comments about their position or atmosphere. Occasionally the most interesting features of a church or graveyard may lie outside the scope of this book as outlined above. The gazetteer features Ordnance Survey grid references (these are the two letters and six digits which appear after each place-name and dedication) and is intended to be used in conjunction with O.S. 1:50,000 scale maps. These are vital for finding churches in urban or remote locations.

Plans redrawn from originals in the author's field notes are reproduced to a common scale of 1:400. The buildings were measured in metres and only metric scales are given. For those who feel a need to convert three metres is roughly equal to ten feet. A system of hatching common to all the church plans in the books in this series is used to denote the different periods of work. On some pages there may be insufficient space for a key to the hatching to be shown. Where this is the case refer to another page. The plans should be treated with some caution. Some features are difficult to date and others are not easy to depict on small scale drawings, such as stones of one period being re-used in a later period, sometimes in a different place.

ABOUT THE AUTHOR

Mike Salter is 46 and has been a professional author-publisher since he went on the Government Enterprise Allowance Scheme for unemployed people in 1988. He is particularly interested in the planning and layout of medieval buildings and has a huge collection of plans of churches and castles he has measured during tours (mostly by bicycle and motorcycle) of all parts of the British Isles since 1968. Wolverhampton born and bred, Mike now lives in an old cottage beside the Malvern Hills. This other interests include walking, maps, railways, board games, morris dancing, playing percussion instruments and calling folk dances with a ceilidh band.

Interior of Wadhurst Church

CONTENTS

INTRODUCTION

Sussex is a comparatively rich county for structural standing remains of Saxon churches, although relics of items such as crosses or funerary monuments as found in other counties are not common. At Bargham are the last remains of an early structure with the rare feature of a west apse. On each side of the main chamber or nave were small chapels or porticus. A porticus still stands almost intact at what is thought to be an 8th century church at Bishopstone. The other Saxon remains in Sussex appear to be of the first two thirds of the 11th century. In several cases all we have are corners of the nave, sometimes with the characteristic long-and-short arrangement of the quoins, and perhaps the odd blocked window above a later arcade. Bosham has a west tower and an impressive chancel arch with a roll-moulding, whilst Worth has a complete cruciform church with an apsed or round-ended chancel and side compartments, which although lower than the nave, are large enough to be considered as proper transepts. A church at Lewes has a re-set doorway and there are towers at Jevington and Sompting, the latter famous for its tall gabled pyramidal roof, a type found in Germany but otherwise unique in England. At Worth, Woolbeding and Sompting are very thin vertical pilaster strips, purely decorative, but recalling the wooden framing of earlier timber churches.

Saxon churches were dark inside, being lighted only by small round headed windows set mid-way through the wall thickness in the earlier buildings but with the openings usually flush with the outer wall-face by the 11th century. The windows were set high up for 11th century naves tend to be tall in relation to their width. Bell-openings in Saxon towers often have two lights with a short shaft between them but Worth is the only known instance of such openings being used in the nave. Saxon churches had fonts, although little remains of them, but contained few other furnishings apart from an altar of stone or wood at the east end of the small compartment built to contain it, called the chancel. Other altars were sometimes provided, especially where there were porticus or transepts containing side-chapels.

Saxon church at Bishopstone

Amberley Church

Newhaven Church

There were evidently plenty of Saxon masons available in Sussex at the time of the Norman invasion of 1066 and the evidence suggests that they were kept hard at work without any break caused by the political changes and the removal of the seat of the bishop to from Selsey to Chichester in 1075. This period is known as the Saxo--Norman overlap, since there are many buildings which are likely to have been built after the Normans took over, but using the skills of Saxon craftsmen. Over a hundred churches in West Sussex have masonry remaining which is likely to be from the period 1000-1125. Dating these buildings more accurately is difficult unless doorways or windows remain. Some of them have patches of walling where stones are laid in alternate rows of about 45 degrees, producing what is known as herringbone masonry. These probably date from c1050-1100. The churches of East Sussex have seen a greater amount of later rebuilding so less early medieval work survives in them, although more than half still have at least one remaining feature dateable to before the year 1200. In West Sussex more than two-thirds of the churches have work earlier than 1200, a high survival rate resulting from populations in remote Downland settlements having stagnated or fallen rather than risen.

Buildings of note dating from the late 11th century are Stopham, which retains original doorways, and Stoughton, with a roll-moulded chancel arch. Stoughton is cruciform but the transepts still open off the nave without a crossing with a tower raised above it as became the fashion for monastic churches and cathedrals, although this form of layout was rarely seen in parish churches before the 1120s. Wisborough Green has remains of a huge early tower which later became part of the nave and Steyning has three fine arches remaining of a central tower and transepts of c1100.

Selham Church

Clymping Church

The first churches in Sussex which are stylistically mature Norman rather than Saxo-Norman overlap were begun in the 1120s. Walls are now thicker than before and windows gradually tend to get larger, at least in the major buildings. The naves at New Shoreham and Boxgrove are reduced to mutilated fragments but there is a complete church at Shipley with a long nave, central tower and chancel. The chevron ornament appears and is widely used until the 1190s, as at Amberley, Burpham and East Lavant. Particularly fine buildings are the nave at Steyning and the crossing tower at Old Shoreham. Towers of the 12th century are quite common in Sussex and often lie in a position other than the usual location at the west end of the nave. Rye had a huge cruciform Norman church but not much now remains of it. Norman central towers remain at Rottingdean and Newhaven, whilst there is a south transeptal tower with ornate windows at Clymping. Newhaven also has an apse. These do not often survive because later generations preferred square-ended chancels and tended to replace them but Up Waltham and Keymer have apses, and there were others that we know of through excavation at the totally destroyed East Sussex chapels of Balsdean, near Rottingdean, and Exceat, near West Dean. North Marden is a very rare single apsed single chamber, never enlarged or seriously altered. Of other smaller churches Tortington is of interest with a good doorway and chancel arch.

East Lavant Church

Bramber Church

Tortington Church

Around 1180 the Norman style began to merge with Gothic forms and the pointed arch came into fashion. The period 1180-1210 is often referred to as Transitional since pure Gothic forms only developed after 1200. Sussex is rich in church architecture of this period. Arcades of plain pointed arches set on piers with Norman style capitals with motifs such as scallops are very common. As populations grew so did the churches. One or two aisles would be added on, chancels were lengthened, and sometimes transepts, towers, and chapels beside chancels were provided. Good examples of the Transitional style can be seen at Boxgrove, where the tower has pointed crossing arches but round belfry arches, other central towers at New Shoreham and Broadwater, the aisled chancel of Shoreham, the chancel of Hellingley, the arcades at Eastbourne and most of the church at Sompting.

East Marden Church

Preston and Up Marden are rare examples of unenlarged and little altered complete 13th century churches of west tower, nave and chancel, and Oving is a larger building with transepts as well, but in Sussex much more common was a 13th century enlargement and remodelling of an 11th or 12th century building. Around 1200 it became the norm for windows to have pointed heads, and the long, thin windows usual in the 13th century are called lancets. Later in the century they were given trefoiled heads and eventually they were grouped together with roundels and trefoils above them to create tracery. Stepped groups of three or five lancets were the norm in the east walls of chancels for most of the 13th century but single lancets were normal elsewhere until at least the 1270s, except occasionally in the belfries of towers. Almost three quarters of the medieval churches of Sussex have at least a couple of 13th century single lancets somewhere in the fabric, most commonly in the north and south walls of the chancel. It was now normal for a piscina to be provided on the south side of the chancel near the east end. This was for rinsing out the chalice after mass. Often set close to it are sedilia, or seats for the clergy. Aisles of the 13th century are very common, although the arcades, usually with double-chamfered arches, are more likely to survive than the original outer walls. These outer walls can be very low indeed in Sussex, where the fashion was for a huge roof coming down close to the ground and covering both nave and aisles in one go, without a clerestory but sometimes with a change of slope where it would be. Findon has the exceptional feature of a roof (actually 15th century) with its apex positioned above the arcade and tie-beams spanning both nave and aisle in one.

Interior of West Tarring Church

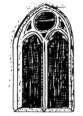

Sedilia at North Stoke   *Window at Petworth*   *Window at North Stoke*

In West Sussex a quarter of the medieval churches never had a tower and made do instead with a timber bell-turret perched on the nave roof. Both bell-turrets and towers in Sussex often have broach-spires, a feature that first appeared c1220 and which continued to remain in fashion in the county, hence the difficulty dating them without conducting scientific tests on the timbers. Elsewhere in England broach-spires are of stone but in Sussex they and the alternative plain pyramidal roofs are normally timber framed with a covering of shingles. In East Sussex the settlements tend to be farther apart from each other and more prosperous. Consequently the churches there are larger on average and nearly all of them have proper towers, although a lot of these towers are of the 14th, 15th and 16th centuries, plus a few that a still more recent. Whilst there are quite a few 13th century towers in Sussex, they tend to be plain and of modest size, as with that attached to the wide single chamber of c1300 at Trotton. Indeed churches in Sussex with notable 13th century work like Clymping, Donnington and Horsham tend to have towers of earlier or later periods. Three towers that should be mentioned here, although two of them are 12th century rather than 13th, are those which are round in plan at St Michael at Lewes, and Piddinghoe and Southease not far to the south. The flints of the Downs were fine for building rough walling but corners required more expensive cut stone from elsewhere. A round plan solved that problem, although it was only in East Anglia that it really took off as an alternative to erecting rectangular towers.

After three centuries of feverish construction since 1000AD most churches in Sussex were as large and grand as they ever needed to be by 1300. Very few newly-founded churches or total rebuildings of existing structures were required in Sussex during the next five centuries until the coastal resorts began to expand in the 19th century and require extra churches. The best work during the long intervening period dates from the 14th century and is found in the ports and in the Weald, for the small churches of the poor hamlets of the Downs generally only required the occasional insertion of a window or two to give just a little more light, or the addition of a modest chapel, porch or tower. Indeed quite a number of the churches, especially in West Sussex, have blocked arcades of 12th and 13th century aisles which were no longer required by the end of the medieval period and so were eventually taken down. Hastings has two large late medieval churches, one late 14th century and the other early 15th century but neither calls for special comment here. Winchelsea has the eastern part remaining of a huge cruciform and fully aisled early 14th century church which was probably never completed. There are aisle-less cruciform late 14th century churches inland at Alfriston and Poynings, whilst Etchingham has aisles but an odd short nave. Harting goes one stage further in having both aisles and transepts, as does the larger and more splendid collegiate church of the 1380s at Arundel. Lindfield has aisles and transepts but the tower lies at the west end. Penhurst is a much more modest building of nave and chancel with a west tower. Much of the heavily restored church at Eastbourne is 14th century, but the arcades are earlier, and most notable feature of the 14th century work is the placing of a vestry behind the main altar.

West Hoathley Church

Work of the 15th century and 16th centuries is not significant in parish churches in Sussex. The contrast with Devon and Cornwall could hardly be greater. Quite a lot of Sussex churches have the odd late medieval window or two, and perhaps a porch or a tower, but there are few instances where this is enough to dominate the character of the church either inside or out. Exceptions are Singleton, with much work of c1400, and Pulborough. A group of towers in East Sussex of this period bears the buckle badge of the Pelham family, but none are of individual importance. East Guldeford is an early 16th century church of brick, but is neither handsome nor left untouched by later alterations. Otherwise brick only occurs in the eastern parts of the church at Herstmonceux.

Arundel Church

Although there are monuments and a few furnishings of the second half of the 16th century in Sussex parish churches, architectural alterations and additions are so sparse nothing calls for mention here. Much of South Malling church is of 1626-8, the forms then used being late medieval. Of more importance are late 17th century rebuildings at Ashburnham and Withyham. The only entirely 18th century buildings are a classical style building of 1763-5 like a Greek temple at Glynde and a late Gothic style building of the 1790s at East Grinstead. A fair amount of St Michael's at Lewes dates from 1748 but little remains of work of the 1740s at Crowborough or of the work of the 1790s at the Chapel Royal at Brighton, but the south side of the small church of c1750 at St Pancras at Chichester retains some original character.

By the early 19th century many of the churches were dilapidated and a fashion for restoration set in. What was done varied considerably according to the whims of the architects and the degree of decay. Sometimes the architecture remained little changed but replacement of the pews, floors, roofs and furnishings changed the atmosphere. Many churches now have mostly 19th century features outside, but the arches inside have often have been little disturbed. Others were treated better and a luckily few in remote areas remained untouched. A positive outcome of restoration was the discovery in a dozen churches of medieval wall paintings later covered over with plaster or whitewash. Apart from continued repairs work of the 20th century is mostly confined to the addition of vestries and meeting rooms plus the rebuilding of half a dozen churches damaged by accidental fires or wartime bombing.

East Grinstead Church

A custom gradually arose of closing off the chancel of a church by a screen with a rood or image of the Crucifixion fixed over it. A dozen or so Sussex churches have medieval screens, most of them 14th century rather than 15th or early 16th century. Some screens had lofts above them for the use of musicians but these rarely survive, although stone access stairs in the outer walls occur occasionally. Chapels were also closed off by screens and again a few of these remain wholly or partly.

Medieval pulpits rarely survive but there is a stone example at Arundel which is part of one of the piers. Elizabethan pulpits are not as common in Sussex as in other counties but there are quite a number of 17th and 18th century examples, including ones with a tester or sounding-board above them. Stalls with miserichords or hinged seats with lips to support a standing person survive in a few of the larger churches, the best ones being at Etchingham. Medieval benches in the nave sometimes remain but slightly more common are 17th or 18th century box pews.

In the medieval period the churches were more colourful than they often are now. Sussex is quite a rich county for remains of wall-paintings in churches. At Hardham Clayton and Coombes enough remains of 12th century decorative schemes to give an idea of what churches of that period originally looked like inside. Sometimes the motifs are purely decorative patterns but mostly they portrayed biblical scenes. These were of importance as a means of conveying God's message to a congregation that was then mostly illiterate and which spoke English in an era when services were conducted mostly in Latin and the ruling classes spoke French. The paintings tend to have long figures with small heads and walls around scenes like play-pens. Preston and Rotherfield have remains of later schemes of c1230 and c1300 respectively.

Old Shoreham Church

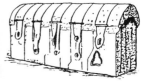

Chest at Warbleton

Roof at Lyminster

Font at Bosham

Font at Eastdean

By far the most likely medieval furnishing in a church to survive restoration was a font. The gazetteers note about thirty as being Norman, i.e. earlier than the 13th century. A common type is square with arcading on the sides, a central stem and four corner columns, and this type continued to be produced into the 13th century, the arcading now having pointed arches rather than round. Other early fonts are tub shaped, either plain or with crude arcading or simple motifs. There is an altogether superior font at Brighton with scenes of figures, another of lesser importance at St Anne at Lewes and there is a lead font of note at Pyecombe. Later medieval fonts tend to be octagonal with quatrefoils or shields on the sides. There are also a number of the Restoration period of the 1660s.

Font at Clymping

Tomb at Winchelsea

Brass at West Grinstead

Three dimensional effigies are not as common in Sussex as in some other counties and the parish churches contain only about two dozen earlier than the 1540s. In addition there are quite a number of empty tomb recesses of the 13th and 14th centuries and the generation just prior to the Reformation sometimes liked to provide a flat-topped tomb chest in a decorative recess on the north side of the chancel which could also be used as an Easter Sepulchre, as at Brede, Selmeston, Isfield and Herstmonceux. Arundel has a fine collection of 15th and 16th century monuments and there are others of note at Boxgrove, Brede, Burton, Easebourne, Herstpierpoint, Horsham, whilst Slindon has a 16th century wooden effigy. Incised slabs are very rare in Sussex and there are few examples of coffin lids with incised or raised floriated crosses. Brasses, on the other hand, are common, partly since although the engraving was done in England the metal had to be imported from abroad, some of it presumably through the Sussex ports. There are two very fine brasses at Trotton, including England's earliest brass of a female (c1310). Buxted, Cowfold, Etchingham, Herstmonceux have other fine examples and there are collections at Ardingley, Battle, Pulborough and Stopham.

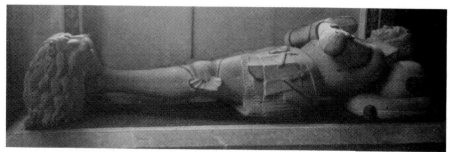

Tomb at Brede

There are a dozen or so tombs with effigies of the second half of the 16th century in the parish churches of Sussex, plus about fifty 17th century monuments, whilst the gazetteers include more than sixty 18th century monuments. Monuments of the period 1550 to 1650 often have effigies on a tomb chest with a coffered arch above. In the medieval period effigies were always recumbent but now they are found reclining or kneeling in prayer, as at Friston, Slaugham and West Dean, and couples are accompanied by small kneeling figures of numerous children. One particularly impressive monument at Chiddingley has standing figures flanking a recumbent pair. The emphasis on effigies gradually decreased during the 17th century, and by the end of that period the most common type of monument was a wall tablet with an inscription (sometimes lengthy) with or without an architectural surround, urns, cherubs, mourners, symbols of death or a profession or a claim to fame. Tablets with frontal busts of the deceased appear in the mid 17th century at Berwick and Ringmer. There are collections of these at Chiddingley, Petworth and Willingdon. With the Weald being an early iron producing area it comes as no surprise that churches there contain 17th and 18th century cast iron memorial slabs in their floors. They are usually plain, with inscriptions across them in large raised letters.

Brass at Crawley

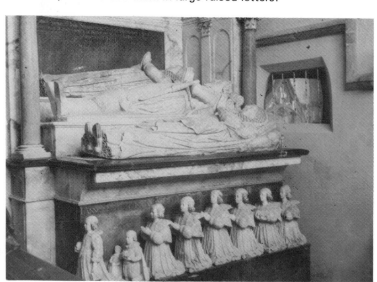

Tomb at Isfield

GAZETTEER OF CHURCHES OF EAST SUSSEX

ALCISTON   *Dedication Unknown*   TQ 505056

The nave NE corner is Norman and there is a small window of that date nearby in the chancel. Further east the chancel has two 13th century north lancets and traces of a third in a position suggesting the chancel was then longer than it is now. Also 13th century is the reset outer arch of the north porch. The roof was rebuilt in 1898.

ALDRINGTON   *St Leonard*   TQ 266053

The tower base is a relic of a medieval church here that lay ruinous until restored and given a south aisle in 1878 by R.H.Carpenter. The nave was rebuilt larger in 1936.

Saxon quoins at Arlington

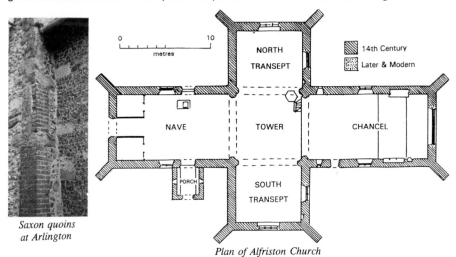

Plan of Alfriston Church

Alfriston Church

Tomb at Alfriston

Saxon window at Arlington

Alciston Church

ALFRISTON   *St Andrew*   TQ 521030

This is a spacious unaisled cruciform church of the 1360s with a central tower and bold diagonal corner buttresses on all four parts. The chancel has an Easter Sepulchre on the north side and ogival headed sedilia and a piscina on the south. The nave now appears shorter than the chancel since its west end is taken up with vestries with a gallery above. The doorways are placed further east than normal and are so close to windows that one of them is slightly obscured by the south porch. The crossing piers have concave sides, even on the capitals. There are no old monuments or furnishings.

ARLINGTON   *St Pancras*   TQ 543075

There is a Saxon window with re-used Roman voussoir tiles in the nave south wall, and three of the corners have Saxon long-and-short quoins, that at the SE later partly rebuilt in brick. The north chapel of c1200 has a pointed arch with dog-tooth towards the nave and round arched north lancets, plus traces of others in the east wall. The arch towards the chancel was replaced in the 14th century by two higher arches with continuous sunk-quadrant mouldings. Of that date also are the renewed east window, the chancel arch, and probably also the king-post roofs. The 13th century west tower is so low that the shingled broach spire starts well below the ridge of the nave roof. The 15th century font is square, an unusual shape for that period, and has panelling. There are very slight traces of wall paintings of foliated crosses on either side of the chancel arch and of St Christopher and St George on the nave north and south walls.

ASHBURNHAM   *St Peter*   TQ 689146

The chancel arch and the embattled west tower with diagonal buttresses and a west doorway with the Pelham family badge of a buckle on the label stops are 15th century. The rest was entirely rebuilt in 1665 although the arches between the chancel and the north and south chapels may be older. The three bay nave is unaisled and has a porch on the north side, wide three-light windows and a panelled wagon roof. The contemporary furnishings include a panelled pulpit, the west gallery on Ionic columns, box pews, a font with a white marble bowl and the communion rail with dumb-bell balusters. The south chapel contained the family pew of the Ashburnham family. In the north chapel are fine monuments in the Baroque style to John, d1671, builder of the church, and William, d1675. John is shown in 16th century style armour between his wives. William is shown kneeling beside the semi-reclining figure of his wife, the Countess of Marlborough.

BARCOMBE   *St Mary*   TQ 418143

The Norman nave and the 13th century chancel are undivided. The chancel was refaced in 1879-80 when the south aisle was rebuilt but the nave retains a 13th century lancet, two 15th century windows and a doorway of c1400 on the north side, and there is a 14th century arcade of two bays with a third older and narrower bay to a former transeptal chapel further east. The low west tower with a shingled broach spire is 13th century but has a 14th century west doorway. The square font with tracery on the sides is 14th century and there is a book cupboard dated 1682 with the names of churchwardens Thomas Earle and John Moore. There is a tablet with caryatid maidens to Susannah Medley, d1730.

BATTLE   *St Mary*   TQ 750158

The church lies north of the abbey and was founded by Abbot Ralph (1107-24). The one remaining feature possibly as early as that is an arch in the north wall of the otherwise chapel, which may originally have opened from a crossing into a former south transept. At the end of the 12th century a longer and wider new nave was built with aisles having five bays of slightly double chamfered pointed arches on piers alternately round and octagonal. There are flat stylized leaves on the capitals and there is a clerestory of lancets set above the spandrels, upon which are a fine series of contemporary wall paintings. In the early 13th century a large new west tower was erected and original crossing was provided with new arches on each side and became the west part of a fine new chancel four bays long with big clasping buttresses on the east corners. In the 14th century a large Lady Chapel was built north of the chancel, with two further arches east of the 13th century one, whilst the south aisle was rebuilt and given a new doorway with a diagonally buttressed porch in the middle bay. Of the 15th century are the present upper parts of the tower, the chapel of St Catherine in place of the original south transept, and the widening of the north aisle to match that of the Lady Chapel, with a rectangular turret containing a staircase to the former loft over the screen. The existing north windows, the chancel east lancets and the chancel arch date from various 19th century restorations, although one north window still has a few fragments of 15th century stained glass.

There is a large square Norman font with seven blank arches on each side. The font cover is 15th century. In a case under the tower are several medieval tiles. There are brasses to Sir John Lowe, d1426, Dean Robert Clare, d1450, and William Arnold, d1435, the latter a small half-figure no longer visible. On a large tomb chest are recumbent effigies of Sir Anthony Browne and his wife who died in 1548.

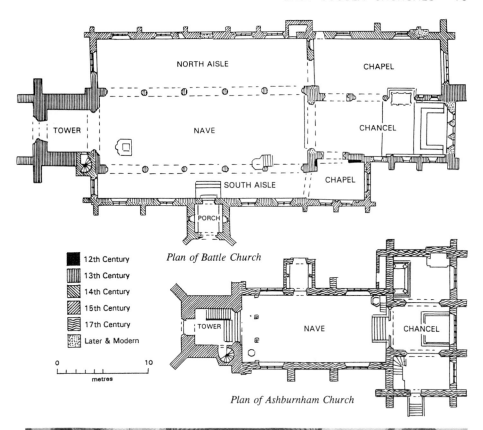

12th Century
13th Century
14th Century
15th Century
17th Century
Later & Modern

0   10
        metres

Plan of Battle Church

Plan of Ashburnham Church

Battle Church

Berwick Church

BECKLEY   *All Saints*   TQ 843237

The west tower is a hotch-potch of several dates. The lower and upper stages are Norman work of two different campaigns. The shingled broach spire may be 13th century. The polygonal NW stair turret and adjacent diagonal buttress are 14th century. The SW buttress, the blocking of the lower north and south windows and the tower arch are 19th century. There are narrow aisles with three bay arcades of double-chamfered arches on octagonal piers, that on the south early or mid 13th century, that on the north of the end of the 13th century. The wider north chapel is 14th century, as are the south porch and the chancel with recticulated tracery in the east window and an ogival-arched piscina, whilst the south chapel is 19th century. The font in use is a fluted oval marble bowl of the 18th century, but there is also a small, damaged, fluted Norman font. Parts of a former late 17th century altar rail with twisted balusters are re-used in the tower arch screen.

BEDDINGHAM   *St Andrew*   TQ 444079

A Norman window survives above the three bay north arcade of c1200 with slightly chamfered pointed arches upon round piers. The south arcade has square abaci to the piers and the arches are unmoulded, with red scrolls and part of a figure surviving of paintings upon them. The chancel is early 14th century unless the trefoil-headed side lancets are slightly earlier. Also 14th century are the clerestory of cinquefoil shaped windows, most of the south aisle walling, and the north aisle east window, the other features of the aisles being Victorian. The tower of flint and stone in an irregular chequer was being built in 1557-9 and has bell-openings typical of that period.

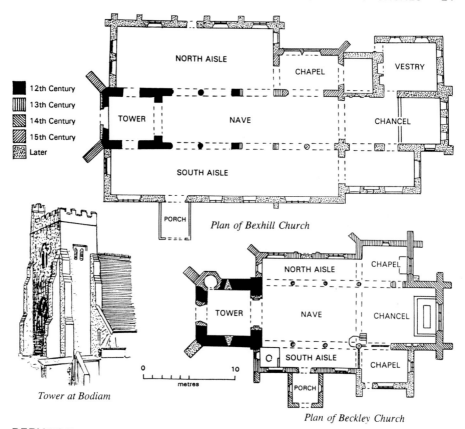

Plan of Bexhill Church

Tower at Bodiam

Plan of Beckley Church

BERWICK   *Dedication Unknown*   TQ 519049

More interesting than the restored medieval features are the wall-paintings of 1942-3. Of the 13th century are the west tower with a shingled broach spire and the chancel windows with rere-arches with shouldered lintels. The chancel north wall contains a 14th century canopy for a former effigy. The south arcade is medieval and there is a monument with frontal busts in oval recesses to John Nutt, d1656, and his wife.

BEXHILL   *St Peter*   TQ 746081

In 1878 a new chancel flanked by a two bay Lady Chapel on the south and a vestry and organ chamber on the north was added beyond the medieval chancel, which then became part of the nave, and the aisles were rebuilt wider than they were before. The nave has arcades of two bays of round arches with slight chamfers, probably of c1180, but the plain narrow arches on either side of the tower look older. Further east each side has a 13th century arch and then the south side has two arches towards a chapel of 1878 and north side has an arch into a chapel built with funds left in 1453 by Lady Jean Brenchley, and used from 1597 as a school. The medieval stained glass figures in the north window here were taken to Strawberry Hill in 1774 as a present from Lord Ashburnham to Horace Walpole, but were later returned. There is a floriated cross-slab and a coped Anglo-Saxon coffin lid with interlace.

BISHOPSTONE   *St Andrew*   TQ 472010

Of an 8th century Saxon cruciform church there remain the nave with two west windows now looking into the tower and a south porticus or small transept. The corners have typical Saxon long-and-short work. The Normans added a west tower with two light bell-openings, a tower arch with a roll-moulding and a pyramidal roof carried on a corbel table with heads, monsters and other motifs. Probably because the tower blocked the original west doorway the porticus was converted into a porch with a projecting south entrance with one order of columns with scalloped capitals and chevrons on the arch. The gable above has a Sundial inscribed Eadric which is thought to be Saxon. The plain inner doorway, set off-centre, is probably the original Saxon arch to the porticus. Also Norman is a square chancel as wide as the nave and having two blank arches on each side. It has two east windows above an arch into a narrower sanctuary. The arches connecting the chancel to the nave and sanctuary have been partly remodelled in the 13th century. The nave has a two bay north aisle of c1200 with slightly chamfered pointed arches. The tiny windows in the aisle look like older openings re-used. The porch contains a 15th century recess with an ogival arch and a frame with fleurons and various Norman carved stones lie here. There is also a Norman coffin lid with three rope-moulded roundels on a shaft containing respectively a cross, the lamb and cross, and two birds drinking from an urn.

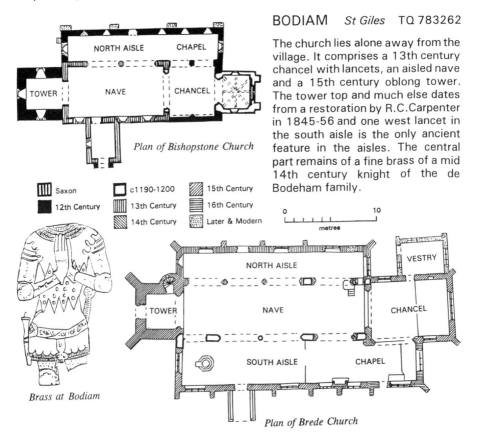

Plan of Bishopstone Church

▥ Saxon	▢ c1190-1200	▨ 15th Century
■ 12th Century	▥ 13th Century	▧ 16th Century
	▨ 14th Century	▦ Later & Modern

Brass at Bodiam

BODIAM   *St Giles*   TQ 783262

The church lies alone away from the village. It comprises a 13th century chancel with lancets, an aisled nave and a 15th century oblong tower. The tower top and much else dates from a restoration by R.C. Carpenter in 1845-56 and one west lancet in the south aisle is the only ancient feature in the aisles. The central part remains of a fine brass of a mid 14th century knight of the de Bodeham family.

Plan of Brede Church

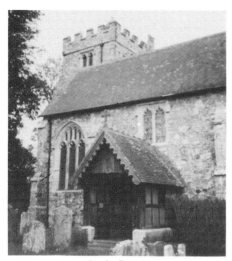

Brede Church

Porch at Bishopstone

BREDE   *St George*   TQ 825183

The narrow arch in the nave SW corner may have once led to a Norman SW tower. Of c1200 is the two bay south arcade with pointed arches with chamfers and a round pier. The three bay north arcade is of c1300 and then north and south chapels were added. The solid wall separating the single arch to each from the older arcades shows where the Norman chancel arch lay. In the 15th century the church was extended by adding a new chancel further east and much of the exterior was rebuilt and a low embattled west tower with a beacon turret was added. One window over the porch contains glass of this period. A round arch on the south side of the new chancel contains a plain contemporary screen and leads into a chapel of the 1530s with an east window with Flamboyant style tracery and fragments of contemporary glass. The chapel was built by Sir Goddard Oxenbridge, d1537, to whom there is an effigy. Only the lower part of the brass of his ancestor Robert, d1482, now remains, although Robert's wife's figure remains intact. These are now set in the back wall of a tomb recess with a projecting tomb chest and a panelled top. The octagonal font with plain arched panels alternating with shields is 15th century.

BRIGHTLING   *St Thomas Becket*   TQ 684210

The chancel and north chapel are 13th century with a two bay arcade between and one original lancet on the north side. One north window is 15th century, otherwise their buttresses and windows are 14th century. The nave south wall is 13th century but with 14th century windows and a porch dated 1749 with flint figures set in a quatrefoil. The north aisle is 14th century but the arrangements are peculiar with a three-quarter arch at the east end. The 13th century west tower has blind arches inside. The west doorway, the boldly projecting diagonal buttresses and the battlements are 14th century. The nave has an old wagon roof. The pulpit and west gallery are 18th century. There are brasses to a 15th century civilian and wife and to the boy Thomas Pye, d1592, and several 17th and 18th century cartouches. In the churchyard is Mad Jack Fuller's large pyramidal mausoleum of 1810.

BRIGHTON   *St Nicholas*   TQ 308045

The church lies above the modern town centre. By far the best feature is the drum-shaped font of the 1160s depicting the Last Supper, scenes of the life of St Nicholas, and the Baptism of Christ. The quality of the carving reflects the fact that the church was under the control of Lewes Priory. The church itself was heavily restored by R.C.Carpenter in 1853 and the clerestory was built in 1892 so the exterior is mostly Victorian. Of the 14th century are the five bay arcades with octagonal piers, the arch from the chancel to the south chapel, and the low diagonally buttressed west tower.

BRIGHTON   *Chapel Royal*   TQ 312043

This church was founded in 1793 but it was mostly rebuilt in 1882 to a design by Sir Arthur Blomfield. It looks more like a Nonconformist chapel, being of brick and terracotta with square corner tower.

St Nicholas' Church, Brighton

BURWASH   *St Bartholomew*   TQ 677248

The west tower of c1100 has two-light bell-openings with scalloped capitals on the central shafts. The south aisle with a three bay arcade and the chancel with several lancets, including three widely spaced ones in the east wall, are 13th century, and the four bay north arcade is 14th century, but most of the windows were restored or inserted in the 19th century. The octagonal concave-sided font is 15th century and has several motifs including the buckle badge of the Pelham family. There is a 14th century cast iron tomb slab with a cross and an inscription to John Colins, the oldest monument of this type in Britain. The other monuments include a small brass of a civilian of c1440 and a cartouche to John Caton, d1675.

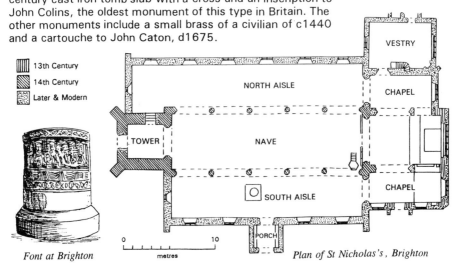

Font at Brighton

Plan of St Nicholas's, Brighton

Interior of Buxted Church

BUXTED   *St Margaret*   TQ 499235

The large church lies in a park away from the village. The west tower is 13th century, but the top is 18th century. The arcades are of four bays, early 13th century with double-chamfered arches on the south, and late 13th century on the north where two of the piers are octagonal and the chamfers of the arches are hollow. The north aisle aisle walling goes with the arcade but the features and porch are 15th century, whilst the wider south aisle is entirely 15th century, as is the rib-vaulted south chapel beyond it. The chancel of c1300 has an original lancet in the middle of each side and a restored east window with cusped intersecting tracery. The sedilia and piscina may be contemporary with the canted ceiling of c1600. The clerestory could also be of that period. The organ-chamber and the outer part of the transept taking the place of the north aisle east bay are Victorian.

The square Purbeck marble font with blank pointed arches with trefoils and set on five supports is probably late 13th century. Of that period is a fine chest like a shrine with cusped arches on the side and rosettes. The pulpit is Jacobean and the altar rail is late 17th century. The monuments include a fine brass of the 1390s with a half-figure of Rector Britellus Avenel in ogival head of a cross, a small brass with a half figure of the priest Deonicius Slon, d1485, and a tablet to George Medley, d1796.

CATSFIELD   *St Laurence*   TQ 728134

The Norman nave has some herringbone masonry. The west tower of c1200 has a west doorway with a quadrant moulding and a later shingled broach spire. The chancel and north chapel are 13th century. The neo-Norman north aisle is of 1845.

CHAILEY   *St Peter*   TQ 393194

The chancel with three grouped east lancets and three more widely spaced lancets in each side wall is 13th century, as is the west tower with a shingled broach spire. Some 14th century work remains in the south aisle but most of it dates from 1878-9 when John Oldrid Scott entirely rebuilt the north aisle and provided an outer north aisle beyond it and vestries west of these.

CHALVINGTON   *St Bartholomew*   TQ 519094

The tiny chancel seems to be early 14th century with intersecting tracery with a foiled circle at the top in the east window and pointed-trefoiled lights in pairs under straight hood-moulds in the side windows. The rather wider nave has late 13th century windows, one of which contains some 14th century glass, although the rest are renewed, and north and south doorways of the same period. Over the north doorway are reset fragments of Norman chevron ornament. The east and west walls of the church are tile-hung and there is a weatherboarded bell-turret with a shingled broach-spire.

CHIDDINGLEY   *Dedication Unknown*   TQ 545142

The ashlar-faced 15th century west tower has a stone spire with polygonal pinnacles and a west doorway with shields in the spandrels and the buckle badge of the Pelham family as label-stops. Several windows are also 15th century but the aisles have 13th century west lancets, the south transept or Jefferay Chapel has a transomed Elizabethan east window, and the chancel is of 1864. The three bay arcades and the king-post roof are perhaps 14th century. The late 18th century pulpit has a gothick tester with an ogee cap. In the chapel is a large monument of 1612 with a reclining effigy of Sir John Jefferay, d1578 set above the recumbent effigy of his wife and flanked by standing effigies of their daughter Lady Elizabeth Montagu and her husband Sir Edward Montagu. A small alabaster tablet has kneeling effigies of William Jefferay, d1611, and his wife. There are also monuments to Margaret Jefferay, d1618, and John Bromfield, d1735.

Monument at Chiddingley

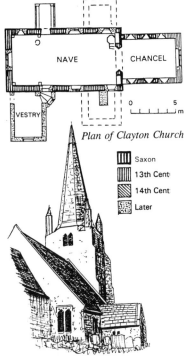

Plan of Clayton Church

▦	Saxon
▦	13th Cent
▨	14th Cent
▦	Later

Chiddingley Church

Clayton Church

CLAYTON   *St John Baptist*   TQ 299140

During a restoration of 1895 by Kempe a fine set of wall paintings of c1140 were discovered on the north, east, and south walls of the nave. The figures and tall and thin with small heads. Over the chancel arch is Christ in an almond-shaped glory with angels and apostles. Below are Christ delivering the keys to St Peter and the book to St Paul. On the north wall are scenes of the fall of the Antichrist, a group of blessed headed by bishops, and the heavenly Jerusalem with three figures inside. On the south are groups of the dammed, the apocalyptic horsemen, the blessed and the Instruments of the Passion.

The nave and west part of the chancel are actually over a hundred years older than the wall-paintings. The chancel has a blocked Saxon north window and there is a chancel arch like that at Worth with semi-circular projections bound by slabs rather than true capitals. There are also traces of small chapels on each side, reached by Gothic arches, now blocked. The chancel has very slim lancets on each side. A wooden bell-turret rises from the roof at the west end of the nave. There is a small brass depicting the priest Richard Idon, 1523.

CROWBOROUGH   *All Saints*   TQ 518306

This church was built in 1744 for Sir Henry Fermor, who is named on the west doorway of the tower, which has keyed-in round bell-openings. The rest of the church was rebuilt for Lord Abergavenny in 1881-3 with round piers and arches and Venetian window tracery. The NW vestry by Teulon has a doorway dated 1897.

CROWHURST   *St George*   TQ 757124

The church was entirely rebuilt at the end of the 19th century by Teulon except for the low west tower with pairs of ogee-headed lights as bell-openings and a west doorway with the Pelham family buckle badge as hood-mould stops.

DALLINGTON   *St Giles*   TQ 658191

A rebuilding of 1864 by Habershon and Brock has left just two 15th century features:
an octagonal font with concave sides and a west tower with a short stone spire set
within an embattled parapet and a west doorway with leaf spandrels.

DENTON   *St Leonard*   TQ 454026

The oldest feature is a Norman tub-shaped font with basket weaving and narrow
bands of pellets above and plait below. The nave has a 13th century north doorway
and the chancel has two lancets of that period. The east window is said to have been
donated in 1368 by a Flemish merchant and the ogee-headed sedile and piscina are
also of about that period. The windows have mostly been restored.

DITCHLING   *St Margaret*   TQ 325153

The nave has Saxon walling and seems small, but the late 13th century crossing
tower has probably taken the place of an original extra east bay. The south aisle with
two pointed arches on plain piers is of c1200. It has a 15th century south porch. The
13th century chancel has three north lancets with shaft with stiff-leaf capitals. There
are also hood-moulds with head label-stops. Tall blank arches flanked the three light
east window, that on the south having a later ogival arch. The 14th century windows
of the Abergavenny chapel on the south side re-use shafted openings from the
chancel south wall. The north transept projects more than the south transept and was
rebuilt in 1863. There is a two-tier tablet to Henry Poole, d1580.

EAST BLATCHINGTON   *St Peter*   TV 484998

What are thought to have been originally a Norman nave and central tower est of it
now form one long nave. The priest's doorway in the chancel could be of c1200 but
the chancel lancets and sedilia and piscina seem slightly later. There is also a 13th
century west tower with a shingled broach spire. The recess of two large blank round
arches in the south wall is thought to be post-Reformation.

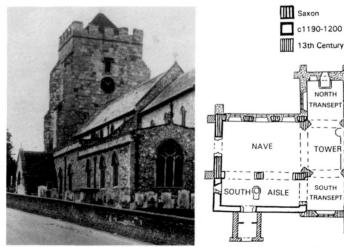

Eastbourne Church   *Plan of Ditchling Church*

Ditchling Church

Tower at East Dean

EASTBOURNE *St Mary* TV 599994

Except for two 15th century windows west of the south porch, the exterior is 14th century, with much 19th century restoration. The large west tower has bold diagonal buttresses and a SE staircase turret. On the north side is a polygonal turret containing a staircase to the former loft over the screen. A passage connects the north porch with the 16th century parsonage beyond. A low vestry projects beyond the chancel east wall. The western bay of each arcade is a 14th century extension but the other four bays in the nave, the three-bay chancel arcades and the chancel arch are all of c1200. The piers are alternately round and octagonal with stiff-leaf capitals. The chancel arch has an outer frieze of crenellation with triangular merlons, whilst to the east it has a frieze of lobes. The easternmost arch on each side of the chancel is no longer open, the 14th century having put an Easter Sepulchre on the north side and sedilia and a piscina on the south side. The other arches in the chancel have 14th century screens with ringed shafts and simple ogival tracery. The square font with angle shafts and panelling on the stem is 15th century. There are Royal Arms of George III painted in 1791. The monuments include a tablet to Katherine Gildredge, d1625, and a bust of Henry Lushington, d1763. East of the church is a Norman cross with a wheel head from St Erth, Cornwall. It once had interlace on the shaft.

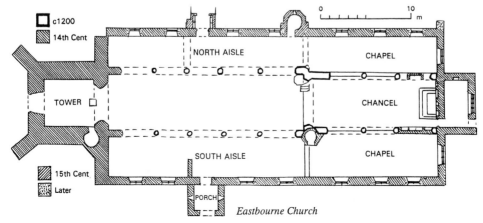

Eastbourne Church

EAST CHILTINGTON   *Dedication Unknown*   TQ 369152

The nave is Norman but the only window of that period now lies in the porch. The short pyramidal-roofed west tower is 13th century. It has a large Victorian west window. Two other windows and the chancel arch are also Victorian. The chancel is 14th century. The font cover is Jacobean and there is a pulpit of 1719.

EAST DEAN

St Simon & St Jude   TV 557977

There was originally an apse on the east side of the Norman north transeptal tower. The chancel has lancets on each side, those on the south having round rere-arches suggesting a date c1200. The nave was lengthened to the west in 1885 and there is a further west extension of 1961. The pulpit and tester are of 1623.

EAST GULDEFORD

St Mary TQ 936215

This brick church begun c1500 and consecrated in 1505 has the unusual feature of twin hipped roofs. Sunk between the roofs is a small bell-turret. Originally the interior was divided by a row of timber posts, removed during a remodelling of c1820, when the present west doorway and windows were inserted. Panels bear the arms of the Guldeford family. The square marble font is earlier than the church and has flat arches on two sides, and three rosettes on the third.

Brass at Etchingham Church

Plan of Etchingham Church

East Guldeford Church

EAST HOATHLY *Dedication Unknown* TQ 520162

Norman relics are a blocked window in the north aisle and the pillar-piscina with chevrons on the shaft. Most of the church was rebuilt in 1856 but the west tower is 15th century and has a higher stair turret and a west doorway with leaves and the arms of the Pelham family in the spandrels, whilst their buckle badge forms label-stops. There are monuments to John Mittell, d1734, and Samuel Atkins, d1742.

ETCHINGHAM *Assumption & St Nicholas* TQ 714262

On the chancel floor are brasses of Sir William de Echyngham, d1389, and his son Sir William, d1412, with his wife and a son who died in 1444. An inscription tells us the older Sir William rebuilt the church, which was collegiate and is known to have been under construction in 1366, whilst a contract of 1369 exists for the making of five windows. The whole structure is of that period and comprises a three bay chancel, and a short two bay nave with a clerestory and aisles extending further east to provide chapels on either side of a central tower. A chapel north of the chancel east end has gone. The windows are mostly of two lights, but the west window and the east windows of the chapels are of three lights and the chancel east window has five lights with flowing tracery, i.e. the style is Decorated rather than Early Perpendicular. The north chapel east window has a segmental head with a band of quatrefoils below which are simple arched lights. The window has the best of several fragments of original stained glass. The tower has a pyramidal roof within a plain parapet and a NE stair turret rising higher. In the chancel are ogival-headed sedilia and a piscina. There is a contemporary chancel screen and the chancel contains stalls with misericords with motifs such as foxes as preachers, two keys, fishes and ladies in late 14th century head-dresses. There are old tiles in the chancel and under the tower. Other monuments include small brasses to Elizabeth Echyngham, d1452, Agnes Oxenbridge, d1480, and the plain tomb chest of Thomas Echyngham, 1482.

Brass at Etchingham Church

Etchingham Church

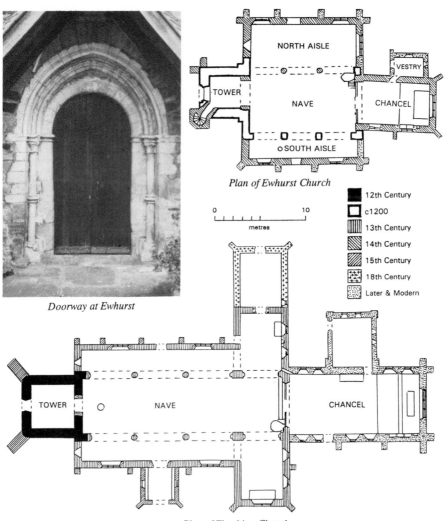

Doorway at Ewhurst

Plan of Ewhurst Church

0   10

metres

■	12th Century
□	c1200
▦	13th Century
▧	14th Century
▨	15th Century
▒	18th Century
░	Later & Modern

Plan of Fletching Church

EWHURST   *St James*   TQ 796246

The three bay south arcade with round arches on square piers with stop-chamfers is Norman. The NE respond suggests there may have been a Norman north aisle also, but the existing much wider aisle here now is late 13th century, with double-chamfered arches on octagonal piers and a west respond carved with a man holding his ears. The chancel is 14th century, but the sedilia and piscina are Victorian, as are the east walls and buttresses of both aisles and the vestry. The fine west doorway with an order of shafts with rings and stylized leaf capitals dates the tower to the 1190s although the buttresses and shingled spire are later. The 13th century font has a shallow square bowl with tapering sides, ornamentation in the spandrels and a round base with spurs. There is a brass to William Crysford, d1520.

FLETCHING   *St Mary & St Andrew*   TQ 428235

Of the Norman church there remain the west tower with two-light bell-openings and two south windows of the nave at different levels above the south arcade. There are 13th century aisles with west lancets and arcades of three wide bays with double-chamfered arches. A fourth arch on each side further east opens into transepts, also with lancets, although the south transept south window has Geometrical tracery closer in date to 1300. The chancel with Kempe stained glass and north vestry date from 1880. The aisle windows and the south porch complete with an original inner door, plus the diagonal buttresses of the tower and the rood screen are 15th century. In the late 18th century John Baker Holroyd, first Earl of Sheffield, added beyond the north transept a mausoleum to contain monuments to himself and his family. Also buried there is Edward Gibbon, author of "The Decline and Fall of the Roman Empire". Other monuments in the church itself include a very fine brass of a late 14th century knight of the Dalyngrigge family with his wife under a canopy, two damaged figures from another monument of that period, a brass with a pair of gloves and an inscription to a medieval glove-maker, and alabaster recumbent effigies of Richard Leche, d1596, and his wife. There is a Jacobean pulpit with arabesque panels.

FOLKINGTON   *St Peter*   TQ 561038

This is a single chamber with lancets, a king-post roof, and a weatherboarded bell-turret. The late medieval octagonal font has a panelled stem. There are monuments with putti to Lady Thomas, d1697, and Sir William Thomas, d1720.

FRAMFIELD   *St Thomas Becket*   TQ 495203

The north chapel was founded in 1288 by the former slave Robert de Hempstead. The lower parts of the aisle walls may be of about that period or slightly later. The arcades and chancel arch with a rood-stair doorway north of it are of the rebuilding after a fire in 1509. An older tower survived until it collapsed in 1667. The existing tower is of 1892. The monuments include a brass to Edward Gage, d1595, and his family, and tablets to Frances Warnet, d1622 and Robert Durrant, d1799.

Framfield Church

FRANT   *St Alban*   TQ 590356

Except for the Victorian east window the entire church is of 1819-22 by John Montier with iron used for the late medieval style tracery and arcade piers. The windows contain fragments of 15th century stained glass and there are three iron memorial slabs, one dated 1631, a tablet to Henry Weller, d1720, and a monument to Charles Brown, d1754, and his wife, d1789.

FRISTON   *St Mary*   TV 552982

The eastern part of the nave is thought to be Saxon, the blocked doorway and window on the south side being probably of that period. The south doorway dates from the Norman period, when the nave seems to have been lengthened westwards. A 14th century porch now covers this doorway. The tiny 14th century chancel has blank arches on the north and south sides. The king-post roof of the nave is 15th century. From it rises a tile-hung bell turret. On the north side is a transeptal chapel with Victorian features but probably an earlier origin which contains monuments of the Selwyns of Friston Place. They include brasses of Thomas, d1539, and his wife, kneeling alabaster figures of Sir Thomas, d1613, and his wife, and a reredos type monument with half pilasters and a segmental pediment to Edward, d1704.

GLYNDE   *St Mary*   TQ 456093

This small rectangular box in the Grecian style with pedimented gables was built in 1763-5 probably to a design by Sir Thomas Robinson. It has a pedimented west porch, three arched windows above an ashlar plinth on each side, and a Venetian east window. The interior has a white coved ceiling with a Rococo cartouche and original box pews, west gallery, pulpit, baluster font and altar rail. The windows have panels of 16th and 17th century glass from the Netherlands, plus Kempe glass in the Holbein style which does not harmonise with the rest of the church.

Glynde Church

Friston Church

GUESTLING   *St Laurence*   TQ 855145

The Norman west tower has a west doorway with one order of columns with scalloped capitals and a roll-moulding, two-light bell-openings and a staircase in a turret clasping the NW corner. The four corners survive of an older Norman nave. A north chapel with lancets and a clasping NE buttress and two bay arcade with chamfered round arches was added c1200. The west window remains of a north aisle which had been added before then, since the chapel has a west arch towards it. The sedilia dates the chancel as 13th century, although the east window is Victorian. Of c1300-50 are the arcades of two bays, the south aisle (though its features are renewed) and the south chapel with a two bay arcade and squint towards the chancel. One north window has fragments of old stained glass. There are kneeling effigies of John Cheyney, d1603, and his wife.

HAILSHAM   *St Mary*

TQ 592096

The church looks late medieval but the south aisle was rebuilt in 1870 and the clerestory is of 1889. The diagonally buttressed west tower has chequerwork of flint and stone, two-light bell-openings with transoms, battlements, polygonal pinnacles and a SE stair turret. The 13th century twin foliage capital in the church is probably from the cloister of Michelham Priory.

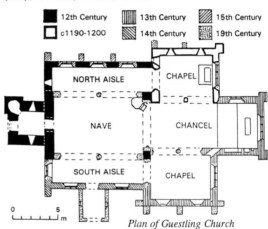

Plan of Guestling Church

Hailsham Church

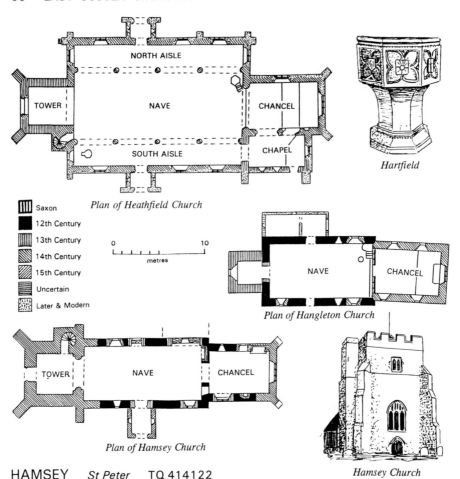

NORTH AISLE

TOWER   NAVE   CHANCEL

SOUTH AISLE   CHAPEL

Plan of Heathfield Church

Saxon
12th Century
13th Century
14th Century
15th Century
Uncertain
Later & Modern

0   10
metres

Hartfield

NAVE   CHANCEL

Plan of Hangleton Church

TOWER   NAVE   CHANCEL

Plan of Hamsey Church

Hamsey Church

HAMSEY   *St Peter*   TQ 414122

The church lies alone at the end of a lane except for one farm. The nave and chancel are both Norman, each having doorways of that period and one window. The narrow chancel arch is flanked by an altar recess on the north and a squint on the south. Of the 13th century are several windows and the blocked arch to a former north chapel. The chancel east end is 14th century and of the end of that period is the broad west tower with diagonal buttresses and a NE stair turret. The south porch is 15th century, as is the octagonal font with cusped panels. One south window contains fragments of old glass. In the chancel is the tomb recess of Edward Markwick, d1538.

HANGLETON   *St Helen*   TQ 267074

The church lies on the side of an estate with a green to the south. The nave has 11th century herringbone masonry and two tiny windows. The west tower is 13th century and the chancel with trefoiled lancets is 14th century, but the east window much more recent. The chancel inclines to the south and has no chancel arch. A 16th century monument has small kneeling figures in a large and decayed frame.

All Saints' Church, Hastings

Hangleton Church

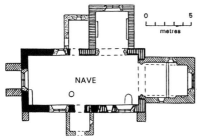

Friston Church

Hartfield Church

HARTFIELD   *St Peter*   TQ 480357

The north wall may be Norman. It contains a blocked late 13th century trefoil-headed lancet. The south aisle and arcade with octagonal piers and double-chamfered arches are 14th century and the nave roof with tie-beams and king-posts could also be that old. The 15th century west tower has angle buttresses and a lofty shingled broach-spire. The octagonal font has pointed quatrefoils with shields.

HASTINGS   *All Saints*   TQ 829098

This church lay at the NE end of the medieval town and is some distance from the modern shopping areas. A will of 1435 refers to it as new and the probability is that it is all of that date although the windows and vestries mostly date from a restoration by Butterfield in 1870. The church is quite large but plain, especially outside, except for some flint and stone chequerwork on the diagonally buttressed west tower where there is a quatrefoil frieze between the west doorway and the window above. The bell openings of two lights are tall with a transom. The east window is of five lights, the others of three and there are original sedilia and a piscina in the chancel. The nave has arcades of four bays of moulded arches rising from octagonal piers. There is a wall painting of the Doom over the chancel arch. The monuments include an incised slab of 1458 depicting a merchant and his wife with signs of the Evangelists in the corners, and brasses of c1520 of Thomas Goodenough and his wife.

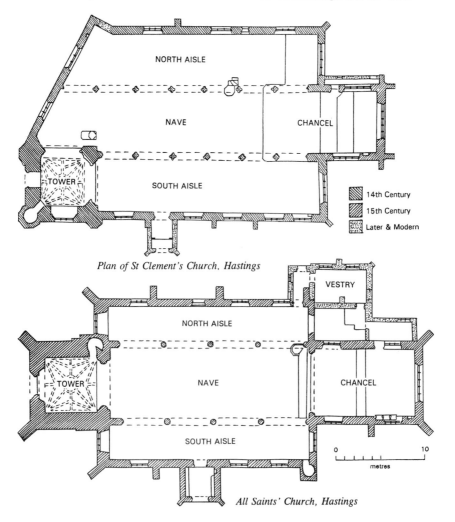

Plan of St Clement's Church, Hastings

All Saints' Church, Hastings

Old print of St Clement's Church, Hastings

HASTINGS   *St Clement*   TQ 825095

This is a wide, spacious church probably of the 1380s and 90s, the original church having been burnt during the French raid of 1377. The site is rather cramped and has led to an odd layout at the west end with the tower positioned at the west end of the south aisle and the west wall of the nave and north aisle set at an awkward angle because of the presence of a road beyond. The north arcade has seven bays, the south only six because of the tower, the piers having four shafts and four hollows. The chancel projects one further bay to the east and is undivided from the nave. The low tower has a tierceron-star vault, a west doorway, polygonal angle buttresses and flint and stone chequerwork. There are leaves on the capitals of the arch towards the nave. The two large two-tier chandeliers were given to the church in 1763. The only monument of note is a tablet to John Collier, d1760.

Heathfield Church

HEATHFIELD   *All Saints*   TQ 599203

The church lies at Old Heathfield and has been restored to the point where only the tower has medieval masonry visible outside. It has a shingled broach spire and is late 13th century but the diagonal buttresses and SE stair turret are 14th century. A little 13th century walling remains in the south chapel. The chancel and the aisles with four bay arcades of double chamfered arches on octagonal piers with a clerestory of quatrefoiled circular windows over the spandrels are all 14th century.

HELLINGLEY   *St Peter & St Paul*   TQ 581124

Of c1200 are the east respond of the north arcade, probably originally part of one arch of a crossing tower, and the fine chancel with the lancets shafted internally with rings and crocket-capitals and a palmette frieze below sill level. The late 13th century north transept has part of a round Norman font with foliage built into the walling. The south aisle and the four bay arcades with octagonal piers are 14th century. The west tower with Y-tracery in the bell-openings and the south aisle SW corner are 18th century. There is a fine brass of a lady in a horned head-dress of c1440.

HERSTMONCEUX   *All Saints*   TQ 644102

The NW tower with clasping corner buttresses and lancet bell-openings flanked by other blank lancets is of c1190-1200, and the two bay north arcade with double-chamfered arches and an octagonal pier goes with it. The three bay south arcade with stiff-leaf on the pier capitals is early 13th century, but the aisle and porch are 14th century, as is the blocked nave west doorway. At the same time as the brick castle was under construction in the 1440s the same materials were used to add a north chapel and rebuild the chancel east wall. In the middle of the chancel floor is a fine canopied brass figure of Sir William Fiennes, d1402. On a canopied tomb between the chancel and chapel are recumbent effigies thought to have originally been placed in Battle Abbey to represent Thomas, Lord Hoo, d1455, and Sir Thomas Hoo, d1486, but moved here c1540 to represent Thomas, Lord Dacre, d1533 and his son Sir Thomas Fiennes. The Norman font was later given some Gothic panelling.

Hooe Church

HOLLINGTON   *St Leonard*   TQ 786114

The chancel was rebuilt in 1865 and the features of the nave are mostly Victorian. A tile-hung bell-turret with a pyramidal roof rises from the nave roof.

HOOE   *St Oswald*   TQ 683022

The church lies alone at the end of a lane. Part of the chancel north wall is Norman. Adjoining it is a square chapel of c1200 with long round-headed lancets and a polygonal east apse later rebuilt in brick. This may have been the lowest stage of an intended tower. The existing tower with diagonal buttresses and a higher NW stair turret is 15th century, as is the wide nave, the south porch and most of the chancel. Several of the south windows have heads on the label-stops. The east window contains original glass showing the Coronation of the Virgin. The pulpit has a fine inlaid tester of c1700. Slightly earlier is the altar-rail.

Plan of Herstmonceux Church

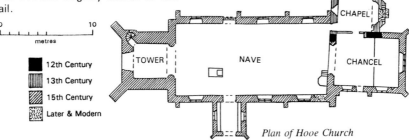

0 _____ 10
metres

■ 12th Century
▥ 13th Century
▨ 15th Century
▧ Later & Modern

TOWER   NAVE   CHAPEL   CHANCEL

Plan of Hooe Church

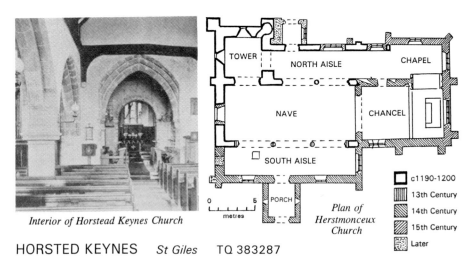

Interior of Horstead Keynes Church

Plan of Herstmonceux Church

☐	c1190-1200
⦀	13th Century
▨	14th Century
▨	15th Century
▦	Later

HORSTED KEYNES   *St Giles*   TQ 383287

This was a Norman cruciform church with a central tower but the north transept has gone and the present south transept is 13th century, when the chancel was remodelled with lancets, including a stepped group of three at the east end. The crossing has a round arch into the chancel and lower round arches to the north and south so the original transepts were more like small and low Saxon porticus. The west arch is 14th century, and probably also of that date is the east arch of the north arcade otherwise rebuilt in 1880. In the chancel is a tiny effigy of a late 13th century cross-legged knight. There is also a small brass of an early 15th century lady and a tablet to Richard Wyatt, d1753.

HOVE   *St Andrew*   TQ 286048

The church was essentially rebuilt in the 1830s by Basevi and has no features or monuments earlier than that period. It is neo-Norman, but with lancets in the chancel.

Interior of Icklesham Church

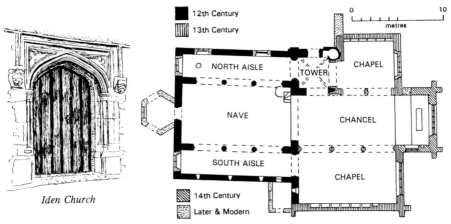

12th Century
13th Century

0   10
metres

NORTH AISLE

TOWER

CHAPEL

NAVE

CHANCEL

SOUTH AISLE

CHAPEL

14th Century
Later & Modern

Iden Church

Plan of Icklesham Church

ICKLESHAM   *All Saints*   TQ 881165

By the mid 12th century what was originally a nave and chancel church had been enlarged by the addition of aisles with three bay arcades with round piers with scallop capitals, a north transeptal tower with a rib vault and north doorway, and a south transept. The last was later swept away by the addition of a large south chapel of St Nicholas in the 14th century when the present east end of the chancel was built. This chapel has a three bay arcade and re-used Norman arcading in the south wall. The tower has Norman arches towards both the north aisle and an almost square north chapel of c1200 with arcading on the north wall and a two bay arcade towards the chancel.The east window and the very unusual hexagonal west porch date from the restoration of 1848-9 by S.S.Teulon. The porch was actually a conversion from a round porch of 1785.

Blocked arches of former south arcade at Icklesham

IDEN   *All Saints*   TQ 916238

Three corners of the Norman nave survive. Aisles with arcades of two bays were added c1200. The south aisle was demolished in the 16th century although the arcade arches can still be seen in the wall. The north arcade was rebuilt except for the responds in the 14th century, whilst the aisle, which is widest at the west end, was rebuilt in the 15th century. Also 15th century are the diagonal buttresses and SE stair turret added to a west tower of c1200, and the north chapel as large as the 13th century chancel, with an arcade of two narrow arches between the two. The chapel seems to have been heightened in the 18th century. The south porch and north vestry are 19th century. There is a brass to the priest Walter Seller, d1427.

IFORD   *St Nicholas*   TQ 408074

The Norman church comprised a nave, central tower and probably an apse. At the end of the 12th century the tower walls were thickened internally, creating blank arches to north and south, a new chancel with triple round-headed east lancets replaced the apse and a north aisle was added. The pointed arches with a slight chamfer are now blocked and contain modern windows matching those of the rebuilt nave south wall. One smaller window on each side at the east end, however, is 14th century. A north chapel was added c1300. Its arch now opens into a Victorian vestry. The cauldron-shaped font on five supports is 13th century.

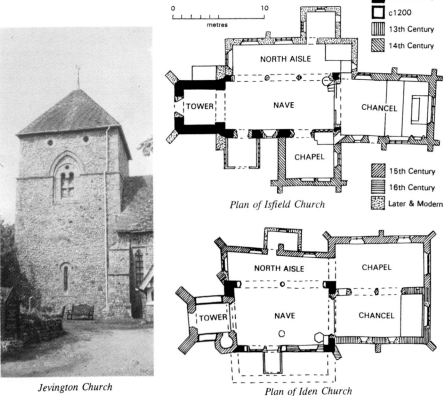

0 _____ 10
metres

■ 12th Century
□ c1200
▦ 13th Century
▨ 14th Century
▧ 15th Century
▤ 16th Century
▒ Later & Modern

Plan of Isfield Church

Jevington Church

Plan of Iden Church

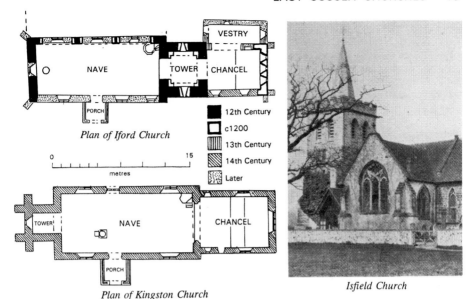

Plan of Iford Church

■ 12th Century

□ c1200

▦ 13th Century

▨ 14th Century

▦ Later

Plan of Kingston Church

Isfield Church

ISFIELD   *St Margaret*   TQ 444182

The church stands alone at the end of a lane, although there are castle earthworks to the west of it. Although the top is Victorian and the diagonal buttresses are later medieval, the tower is essentially Norman, with wide original windows. The north aisle and the vestry beyond it are of 1876. The south doorway, the south chapel and the chancel connected by a squint are all early 14th century. The nave south lancet between the timber porch and the chapel, however, must be 13th century. The chancel is wider than the nave and has a gabled piscina, whilst sedilia are formed in a window embrasure. The chapel has original glass in the south window and contains monuments to the Shurley family. There are tomb chests in recesses to Sir John, d1527, whose brass is now missing, and to Edward, d1558, whose brass survives. There are also brasses of Thomas, d1578 and his wife, and a large ashlar monument with a deep coffered arch, columns, and recumbent effigies of Sir John, d1631 and his two wives, with their children kneeling at the side.

JEVINGTON   *St Andrew*   TQ 562016

The pyramidal-roofed west tower is Saxon. Above the bottom lancets (which are ancient but renewed) are blocked windows with Roman tiles re-used as voussoirs. The bell-openings are renewed but represent what was there except that each now has the outermost arch pointed instead of round, and the roundel opening above the central turned baluster shaft is not ancient. The south doorway is of c1200 and the north aisle with small renewed lancets and an arcade of double-chamfered arches and a round pier is not much later. The nave has a 16th century roof with alternating king-posts and hammer-beams. Fixed on the north wall is a Saxon tablet showing the risen Christ in a loin cloth thrusting a cross-shaped sword into the mouth of a dragon. The is much renewed but has a 14th century piscina and aumbry. The squints into it were made straighter in the restoration of 1871-3. The font is thought to be of c1400, but the lead bowl may be older. It has traces of cover fastenings.

KINGSTON   *St Pancras*   TQ 392082

The small buttressed west tower, the nave with two-light windows and north and south doorways, and the chancel are all 14th century. Only the circular moulded 13th century font seems earlier. Some of the windows are renewed but the only later addition is a 19th century timber porch.

LAUGHTON   *All Saints*   TQ 501125

The chancel with an ogival-arched priest's doorway with quatrefoils on the jambs and arch seems late 18th century. The nave has one 13th century lancet on either side. Of the 15th century are the chancel arch and the embattled west tower with the buckle badge of the Pelham family on the label stops of the west doorway. The nave has a single framed roof with tie-beams and king-posts. Parts of the tracery of the medieval rood screen survive against the chancel east wall.

LEWES   *All Saints*   TQ 417101

The church now serves as a youth and arts centre. Only the low west tower with diagonal buttresses is medieval. The brick nave of six bays with windows in two tiers dates from 1806 and the transepts and chancel were added in 1883. Some of furnishings are of c1806 and there are kneeling figures of Robert Hassard, d1624, and John Stansfield, d1627, and their wives, once part of a large monument.

All Saints' Church, Lewes   *Laughton Church*

St Anne's Church, Lewes

LEWES   *St Anne*   TQ 408100

This church in the High Street has a long Norman nave. The doorway is now reset
as the outer arch of a shallow north porch. One original south window remains above
the four bay south arcade of c1185-1200. The arcade has pointed arches with slight
chamfers on round piers with stiff-leaf capitals, but the east bay is round arched. This
corresponds to an older south transept with an original east window now looking into
a Victorian vestry. When the arcade was added the transept was given a rib vault
with a small central boss with stiff-leaf. The west tower is also Norman but has 15th
century buttresses. The chancel has corner corbels suggesting the intention of
vaulting. It is 13th century and contains a later tomb chest with an ogival canopy but
has been much rebuilt. The nave roof with tie-beams, queen-posts and raking struts
is of 1538. The Norman font is drum-shaped with a basket-weave motif with a band
of plait below and pellets above. The pulpit of 1620 has two tiers of panels with
lion's heads and angle columns. The west gallery and altar rail are 18th century.

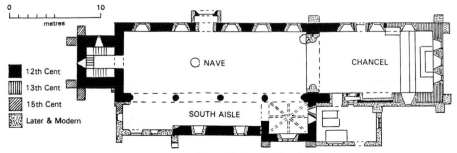

Plan of St Anne's Church, Lewes

St John the Baptist's Church, Lewes   *Saxon doorway at St John-under-the-castle, Lewes*

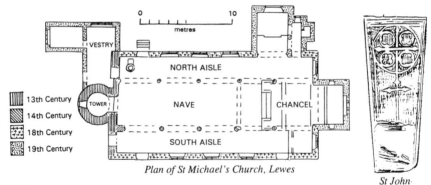

Plan of St Michael's Church, Lewes

St John Lewes

LEWES   *St John Baptist*   TQ 413097

Originally this was a hospital by the main gate of Lewes Priory. The four bay south arcade of unmoulded arches on short round piers may have originally divided the men's part of the hospital from the women's part. The late medieval bay to the east has come from elsewhere. The tower arch may be 14th century but the tower itself with brick chequer below and battlements with a cupola is of 1714-38. The neo-Norman south chapel is of 1847 and the chancel dates from 1885. In two south recesses are cists of lead, relics of the tombs of William de Warenne and his wife Gundrada, founders of Lewes Priory. There is a large black marble slab to Gundrada, made about a century after her death in 1085. The mutilated marble effigy of a late 13th century knight is thought to be John de Braose.

LEWES   *St John-under-the-Castle*   TQ 414105

The existing church of flint with brick dressings and having a tower with castellated turrets is of 1839 by George Cheeseman. Reset on the outside at the east end are three relics of the original church further north. Of the Late Saxon period are the former chancel arch with an inscription referring to a Danish prince called Magnus who became a hermit here and a doorway flanked by three demi-shafts and rolls with a slab across all three instead of proper capitals. The cross-slab is probably later.

LEWES   *St Michael*   TQ 413110

The 14th century three bay south arcade has hollow chamfers on the arches. The pebble-dashed round tower at the west end has a shingled spire and is thought to be 13th century on account of its west lancet although most other towers of this type are Saxon or Norman. In 1748 the church was remodelled as a fully aisled rectangle of five bays, the new arches on the north and east being of wood with octagonal piers and panelled arches. In 1885 the windows were Gothicised, an extra unaisled bay added at the east end, an organ chamber added beyond the north aisle and a vestry provided north of the tower. There are brasses of the priest John Braydford, d1457 (a half figure) and of a 15th century knight (now headless). A tablet has kneeling figures of Sir Nicholas Pelham, d1559 and his wife and children.

LEWES   *St Thomas Becket*   TQ 421104

This church served the suburb of Cliffe, east of the river. Much of the exterior is 19th century except for the 15th century west tower with leaves on the spandrels of the west doorway. Of the 14th century are the arcades with hollow-chamfered arches and a squint with a foiled ogival arch at the chancel end. The clerestory windows were above the spandrels of the arcade arches.

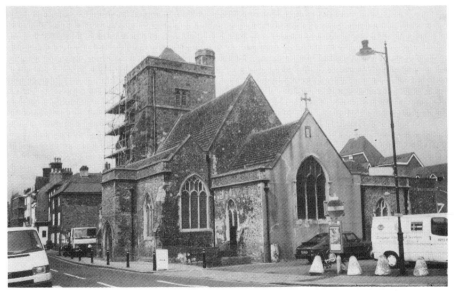

St Thomas's Church, Lewes

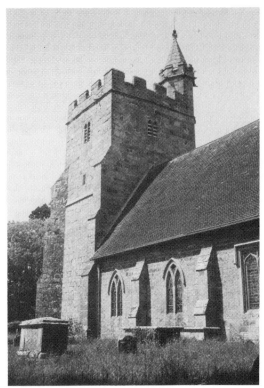

Chancel at Little Horsted

Tower at Little Horsted

LITLINGTON   *St Michael*   TQ 523020

Green man at Little Horsted

In the 14th century the Norman nave with traces of two original north windows was given diagonal west corner buttresses before being extended by a further bay, also with diagonal corner buttresses, to carry a weatherboarded bell turret. The chancel has two Norman north windows, 13th century sedilia, and a roof and Easter Sepulchre recess of the 15th century.

LITTLE HORSTED   *St Michael*   TQ 470184

The Norman chancel has four blank round arches on the north side. Into two of them are set tiny windows. The 15th century ashlar-faced west tower has a polygonal NE stair turret rising higher and a west doorway with a Green Man carved in one of the spandrels. The other features are mostly 19th century.

LULLINGTON   *Dedication Unknown*   TQ 528031

Only traces remain of the nave and the western bay of the 13th century chancel, the other two bays of which remain in use as a chapel. One original north window remains, the other lancets being 14th century. The site is quite hidden away and is reached only by a long winding path.

MARESFIELD   *St Bartholomew*   TQ 466240

The transepts and chancel were built in 1875-9 by J.Oldrid Scott. Re-used 13th century parts in the chancel are the piscina, a small north lancet, and the inner arches of two larger north windows, whilst the arch to the north transept was once the medieval chancel arch. The nave is Norman, with one small original south window and a SW window of the 14th century. Three other windows are 15th century, the period of the diagonally buttressed west tower. A sounding board dated 1621 from the Jacobean pulpit has been made into a table. The altar rail is also of that date.

MAYFIELD   *St Dunstan*   TQ 587270

The church lies west of the former palace of the Archbishops of Canterbury, now a convent. Much of the church dates from after a fire in 1389 but the short west tower and the west lancet of the north aisle are 13th century. The shingled broach spire is later. There are arcades of four and a half bays with four-centred arches on octagonal piers. The south chapel has a fine ceiling with moulded beams. The south porch has a rib vault with a boss and another room above. The outer entrance is triple-chamfered. The Jacobean pulpit has arabesque carving, and there is a font of 1666. Part of the dado of the screen is 15th century. The altar rail is 18th century. The monuments include iron slabs of 1668 and 1708, a tablet to Thomas Aynscombe, d1620, and late 18th century tablets to members of the Baker family.

MOUNTFIELD   *All Saints*   TQ 735203

The nave is Norman, with two original windows and a blocked doorway in the nave north wall. The narrow chancel arch is flanked by two smaller openings of later date. The chancel has three lancets and a priest's doorway of the 13th century, but the walling is probably Norman. The low west tower containing ancient wooden steps and having a shingled broach spire beginning below the ridge of the nave roof is 13th century. The drum-shaped font is Norman but with later medieval carved motifs. The south porch of massive timbers is 14th century and the nave wagon roof may also be of that period. There is an 18th century altar rail.

NEWHAVEN   *St Michael*   TQ 443012

To the east of Habershon's aisled nave of 1854 with timber arcade posts are a Norman central tower and east apse with two pilaster buttresses and one original window. The tower has a west arch with one order of columns facing west and two orders facing east, whilst the east arch also has two orders of columns. There are two-light belfry openings, one with an original shaft with a shaft-ring, and there is a corbel table with heads and monsters. The short shingled broach spire is later.

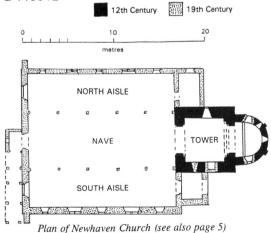

Plan of Newhaven Church (see also page 5)

Newick Church

Litlington Church

NEWICK   *St Mary*   TQ 421208

The west doorway of the diagonally buttressed west tower with a polygonal NE stair-turret has large heads as label-stops. The west half of the nave south wall is Norman, with one window of that date, plus two others and a doorway of the 13th century. In 1886-7 J.Oldrid Scott lengthened the nave eastward, added a new chancel beyond (in the south windows of which are fragments of medieval glass), and provided a wide north aisle. There is a Jacobean pulpit with a tester and also a square font with three blank cusped ogee-headed panels on each side.

NINFIELD   *St Mary*   TQ 705123

The windows of the 17th century chancel and the rendered 13th century nave, plus whole of the north aisle are of 1885-7, and the brick south porch is of 1735. From the nave roof rises a white weatherboarded bell-turret. The font and its cover are probably of the 1660s, whilst the reader's desk and panelling in the chancel could be earlier, and the west gallery reached by a ladder may be slightly later.

NORTHIAM   *St Mary*   TQ 830245

The lower stage of the west tower is Norman with original windows to the north and south. The tower arch was made pointed when the upper stage was added in the 13th century. It has lancet bell-openings set in three-bay blank arcading. In the 15th century the tower was given a recessed stone spire, a west doorway, a heavy NW buttress and a polygonal SW stair turret from which project two buttresses. The aisles are 13th century with three bay arcades of double-chamfered arches and slender round piers, over which are small clerestory windows. The south aisle windows and porch are 14th century which the north aisle windows and buttresses are 15th century, although the west window is 14th century. In 1837 the church was enlarged with a spacious new chancel flanked by three bay chapels wider than the aisles. The work was paid for by Thomas Frewen Turner, who in 1846 added beyond the north chapel a mausoleum designed by Sidney Smirke, in which are 19th century Frewen monuments. The three sided altar rail was donated in 1638 by Thankful Frewen, and the panelling and altar table are of the same date. The 18th century pulpit has a leaf-frieze at the base. The brass chandelier is dated 1727. In the chancel are brasses to the priest Robert Beuford, d1518, and Nicolas Tufton, d1538.

ORE   *St Helen*   TQ 821124 & 821121

Brasses of a civilian and wife of c1400 lie in the new church of 1869 by Habershon and Brock. They have come from the old church, ruins of which lie hidden away in trees by a new estate to the south. The site is somewhat overgrown and little can seen of the 16th century south aisle flanking both the Norman nave and the narrower 13th century chancel with two north lancets flanking a tomb recess. The east window is 14th century and there are later windows in the nave north wall. The west tower of c1200 has clasping west angle buttresses and a spiral stair on the north.

OVINGDEAN   *St Wulfran*   TQ 355036

The east arch remains visible of a former two bay 13th century aisle. The chancel has Norman windows on all three sides and the nave has a Norman north doorway. Modern arches flank the plain round chancel arch. The tower of c1200 has lancets and a pointed arch towards the nave with just a slight chamfer. Towards the south chapel of 1907 the chancel south wall has a pointed blank arch into which open a low-side lancet. There is a plain late medieval screen.

Ninfield Church

Ovingdean Church

PATCHAM   *All Saints*   TQ 303092

The plain chancel arch is Norman and is flanked by reredos recesses perhaps also of that date. Above is much restored early 13th century wall painting of the Last Judgement. Other 13th century features include the thin west tower with lancet bell-openings. The porch and buttresses on the south side are 16th or 17th century. A north aisle was added in 1898 when Brighton suburbia reached this far inland. The damaged monument of Richard Shelley, d1594, features nude grave-diggers.

PEASMARSH   *St Peter and St Paul*   TQ 887218

The Norman nave has an original west window high up now looking into a late 12th century tower with clasping corner buttresses. Also Norman are the west part of the chancel and the three bay arcades, although the eastern bays have nook-shafts of a 13th century looking type. The north aisle has one Late Norman west window but the south aisle was mostly rebuilt in the 14th century. A porch then provided has been rebuilt. Most of the chancel, including the three lancets on each side and the sedilia and piscina, is 13th century, but the east window is 14th century.

PENHURST   *St Michael*   TQ 695166

This small nave and chancel church of c1400 has escaped without much restoration. The nave has a king-post roof and the chancel a wagon roof and there is a contemporary screen, whilst the east window contains fragment of original glass. The 15th century tower with diagonal buttresses and a SE stair turret was never completed to the intended height and now has tile-hanging at the top and a pyramidal roof. The north chapel with a round arch towards the chancel and the pulpit, reader's desk, pox pews and nave panelling are all 17th century.

Pevensey Church

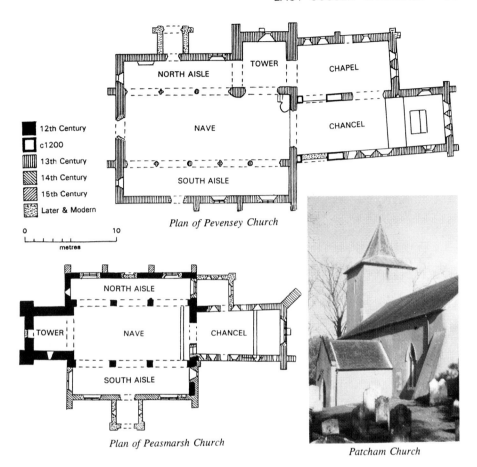

12th Century
c1200
13th Century
14th Century
15th Century
Later & Modern

0   10

metres

TOWER

NORTH AISLE

CHAPEL

NAVE

CHANCEL

SOUTH AISLE

Plan of Pevensey Church

NORTH AISLE

TOWER   NAVE   CHANCEL

SOUTH AISLE

Plan of Peasmarsh Church

Patcham Church

PETT   *St Mary & St Peter*   TQ 873139

The church was rebuilt in 1864 by Benjamin Ferrey and the earliest monument dates
from the 1820s, but there is an octagonal font of 1753 with a fluted baluster stem.

PEVENSEY   *St Nicholas*   TQ 647048

The church is mostly 13th century as one might expect since much of the castle
dates from the 1220s to the 1260s. It comprises a long chancel with several lancets
and inclined to the north from the axis of an aisle nave with a five bay arcade on the
south and on the north a three bay arcade and then a north transeptal tower. The
arcades have double-chamfered arches on piers alternately quatrefoiled and octagonal
and there are clerestory windows set over the piers. There is stiff-leaf carving on the
restored chancel arch. The king-post roof is later. Older than the rest, being probably
of c1200, are the chamfered but otherwise plain pointed arches on either side of the
west bay of the chancel. In the 1870s G.G.Scott Junior rebuilt the bell-stage of the
tower and the spacious north chapel, and added the north porch. There is a reclining
effigy of John Wheatley, d1616, with an alabaster monument with lions on the floor.

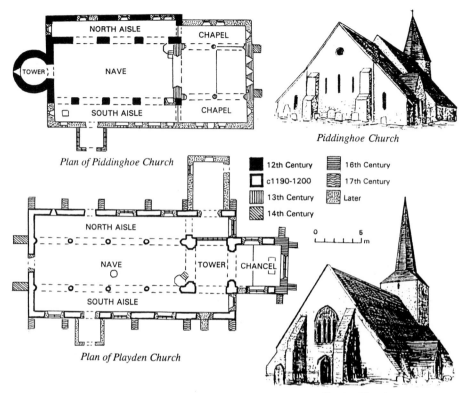

Plan of Piddinghoe Church

Piddinghoe Church

■ 12th Century		▤ 16th Century	
☐ c1190-1200		▨ 17th Century	
▥ 13th Century		▨ Later	
▨ 14th Century			

Plan of Playden Church

Playden Church

PIDDINGHOE   *St John*   TQ 435031

The churchyard lies right beside the River Ouse. The round Norman west tower has a shingled octagonal spire. The narrow and very low north aisle is later Norman, with three unmoulded round arches cut through the older nave wall. The south aisle has been rebuilt but has a similar arches, but of four pointed arches with slight chamfers. The chancel is 13th century and has three east lancets with an oculus above in the gable and a restored original chancel arch. The north and south chapels of the same date were rebuilt in 1882 but their two bay arcades of double-chamfered arches on round piers still remain. The only furnishing of note is a barrel organ of c1820.

PLAYDEN   *St Michael*   TQ 920218

Most of the church dates from the 1190s. It consists of a nave with arcades of four bays opening into aisles which extend further east to flank a central tower, beyond which is a square chancel. The crossing arches are simply stepped without columns. Under the crossing is an ancient ladder. The north doorway with quadrant mouldings is original and west of it is a tiny original window. The west doorway and heavy west buttresses are 14th century, whilst the south buttresses are 17th century and the chancel east end, also buttressed, is 16th century. There is a late medieval screen. The 18th century pulpit has two candle-holders, The barrel on the incised slab with a Flemish inscription to Cornelis Retmans suggests he may have been a brewer.

PLUMPTON   *St Michael*   TQ 356135

The Norman nave has a plain original south doorway and the 13th century chancel has one north lancet, plus two renewed ones on the south, whilst the east wall has been entirely rebuilt. The 13th century west tower with a shingled broach spire has one small lancet but the west doorway and buttresses are 14th century. There are faint wall paintings high up on the north wall, one scene showing Christ seated in the Heavenly Jerusalem. The south porch is 16th century with an 18th century front.

PORTSLADE   *St Nicholas*   TQ 255063

The narrow south aisle with a three bay arcade with plain pointed arches on round piers with scalloped capitals is of c1190. Of the 13th century are the west tower and the chancel with restored sedilia and a sexfoiled window over two lancets in the east wall. The wide north aisle and the chapel west of it containing the Brackenbury family monuments are of 1874. The brass plate in the south aisle to members of the Scrase family who died in 1499, 1519, and 1579 has come from West Blatchington.

PRESTON   *St Peter*   TQ 304064

It comes as something of a surprise to find just 2km north of Brighton an almost unaltered 13th century church consisting of a nave, a much narrower chancel and a thin west tower. It is cared for by the Churches Conservation Trust. There are three renewed lancets in each side of both the nave and chancel and a triple lancet east window. Only the nave west corners have buttresses. Only a timber north porch and a stone vestry built in front of the nave south doorway are later. Prior to the fire of 1906 there was almost a complete set of 14th century wall paintings. Some survive on the nave east and north sides. A tomb chest with shields in cusped quatrefoils used as an altar is thought to be the tomb of Edward Elrington, d1515.

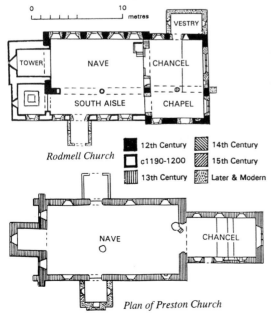

Rodmell Church

■ 12th Century		▨ 14th Century	
☐ c1190-1200		▨ 15th Century	
▥ 13th Century		▧ Later & Modern	

Plan of Preston Church

Preston Church

RINGMER   *St Mary*   TQ 446126

The south chapel is of c1500, although it incorporates a south doorway and window of the 14th century, and the north chapel is of the 1530s but has a Jacobean plaster ceiling with decorated beams. The chapels have two bay arcades of four-centred arches to the chancel. The arcades between the nave and aisles are 14th century but 13th century pier bases remain on the north side. The massive timbers of the south porch are 14th or 15th century. The nave west end and the west tower are of 1884-5 by Ewan Christian. Set into the SW buttress are Norman fragments. On the north side is a 20th century extension. An alabaster tablet has a kneeling figure of Herbert Springett, d1620, and there is a tablet to Sir William Springett, d1643. Other monuments include tablets to Elizabeth Jefferay, c1620, Richard Wynne, d1679, and Ensign Crunden, d1793.

RIPE   *St John Baptist*   TQ 524099

The church is mostly 15th century and has an embattled west tower with the buckle badge of the Pelham family on the doorway. Older features are the restored five-light east window with flowing tracery and fragments of original coloured glass, plus the single sedile. The arch of a second sedile seems to have been used for a later recess beside the chancel arch.

RODMELL   *St Peter*   TQ 412063

The nave and chancel are both Norman, with an original window in the latter, but the arch between them is now Victorian. The south aisle of c1200 has an arcade of two bays with round arches and a circular pier. At each end of the aisle are contemporary arches, one to a square baptistry with one original lancet lying beside the pyramidal-roofed west tower. The other leads to a two bay south chapel probably of c1200-20. The screen under the arcade between chapel and chancel is early 14th century. There is a square font of Purbeck marble with blank arches. One north window contains a 15th century stained glass crucifixion. Two Norman carved fragments lying loose are thought to be from the lavatorium of Lewes Priory.

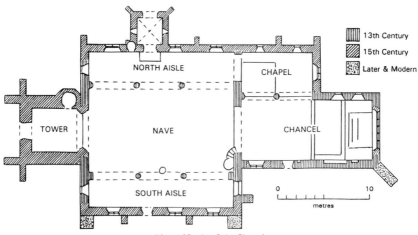

Plan of Rotherfield Church

Ringmer Church

ROTHERFIELD   *St Denys*   TQ 556298

This is quite a large church, dominated by a recessed shingled spire. The three bay arcades of double chamfered arches are 13th century, that on the north having round piers, whilst that on the south has slightly later octagonal piers. The nave is wide, yet the aisles were originally very narrow, their west lancets still remaining. In the 15th century the aisles were widened slightly, a rib-vaulted porch with a room above was added on the north side, a new wagon roof provided and an ashlar faced tower built at the west end with bold corner buttresses and a polygonal NE stair turret. The single-frame roofed chancel and the two bay north chapel are also 13th century, although the five light east window and the north chapel screens are 15th century. Blocked arches in the chancel south wall and the south aisle east wall are the only remaining traces of a tower originally in the corner between the two. The elaborate font cover is dated 1533. There is a fine early 17th century pulpit with tapering pilasters, eagles on the back panel, and a large tester. There are box pews rising up towards the west end of the nave. Over the chancel arch are wall paintings of c1300 depicting Doom with St Michael weighing souls and Christ and angels. Other fragments of wall paintings survive in the north chapel and south aisle. The only monuments of interest are a cast-iron ledger plate in the north aisle and a tablet to Nicholas Fowle, d1656.

Rodmell Church

Rottingdean Church

ROTTINGDEAN   *St Margaret*   TQ 369026

The long nave and the central tower are of 11th or 12th century origin although their earliest features are 13th century lancets and buttresses, plus the priest's doorway and the triple-chamfered east and west arches under the tower. In his restoration of 1856 Sir George Gilbert Scott widened the nave, built a south aisle partly on the site of a shorter 13th century aisle or chapel, and rebuilt the chancel east wall. The bases of original lancets remain below his twin-lancet windows in the nave north wall.

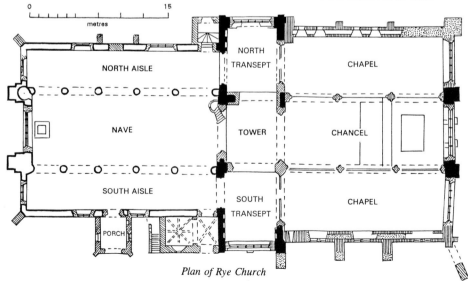

Plan of Rye Church

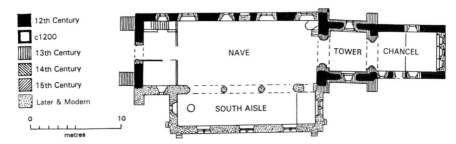

12th Century
c1200
13th Century
14th Century
15th Century
Later & Modern

0   10
metres

NAVE   TOWER   CHANCEL

SOUTH AISLE

Plan of Rottingdean Church

RYE   *St Mary*   TQ 921204

The transepts remain of a cruciform Norman church possibly as long as the present building. The transepts have blank arcading with a crenellation frieze on the north and chevrons on the south. The arches to the aisles are also Norman, but the present aisles are early 13th century. They are of five bays with piers alternately round and octagonal and arches with rolls and chamfers, those to the west being more pointed than the others. The west front has big original buttresses against the responds, 14th century diagonal corner buttresses and large renewed windows. Adjoining the south aisle are a 14th century porch and chapel, both rib-vaulted, with a sacristy above them with circular west window, plus a 15th century porch further west, whilst another 14th century porch in the angle between the north aisle and transept contains a 17th century staircase to the central tower. By the late 13th century the chancel had been provided with wide three bay chapels with lancet windows, those on the south being in pairs with shafts internally and an oculus above. Both chapels have wall passages at the level of the window sills. Apart from the eastern two arches on the north the chancel arcades were rebuilt in the 15th century, the period of the present crossing and tower above. The spirelet and wind-vane are of 1702.

The pulpit has early 16th century linenfold panels. There are late medieval screens between the transepts and chancel chapels. The brass two-tier chandelier is dated 1759. The clock on the north transept which can be seen from the High Street has a framework and quarter-boys of c1760, but the works were made at Winchelsea in 1561-2. The monuments include an urn to Catherine Owens, d1797.

Rye Church

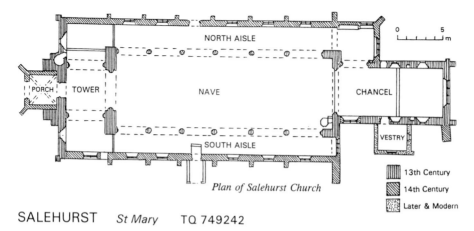

Plan of Salehurst Church

13th Century
14th Century
Later & Modern

SALEHURST   *St Mary*   TQ 749242

This is quite a long 13th century church with a chancel of three bays, arcades of six bays with double-chamfered arches on octagonal piers and a seventh bay on each side flanking the west tower. The west doorway is round headed and has one order of shafts. Except for their west lancets the aisles were rebuilt without being widened in the 14th century. The east window has cusped intersecting tracery of c1300. The 15th century tower top has chamfered corners. The clerestory dates from 1861. There are four salamanders around the 13th base of the font. Two south windows contain old glass. The south also contains the front of a tomb chest with three shields in quatrefoils and the 14th century north chapel has a tomb recess with a crocketed ogival gable. There is a monument to Anne Peckham, d1758, and there are several cast-iron grave slabs and several 17th and 18th century cartouche tablets.

Interior of Seaford Church

SEAFORD   *St Leonard*   TV 482991

Seaford was once one of the Cinque Ports and a major early church is to be expected here. For some strange reason the 14th century west tower was built inside the west bay of a Norman nave. The Norman arches on each side thus blocked cannot have formed part of regular arcades, but there clearly were Norman arcades for although the two bay arcades further east are 13th century, the north aisle has very tiny Norman windows in the outer wall. The arcade capitals are carved with stiff leaves and scenes of the Baptism of Christ, the Harrowing of Hell, Daniel in the Lion's Den, the Massacre of the Innocents, and the Crucifixion. The clerestory is also 13th century, with fine shafted windows. The south aisle is 15th century and does not flank the tower like that on the north does. The tower top is also 15th century. The eastern part of the church with an apse and transepts is the work of John Billing in 1861-2. There is a fine panel of the 1130s showing St Michael with the Dragon.

SEDLESCOMBE   *St John the Baptist*   TQ 777188

Old features which survived the restoration of 1866-74 by Norman and Billing are the 15th century west part of the north aisle with fragments of old glass in one window, the 14th or 15th century embattled west tower with a higher stair turret, a tie-beam dated 1632 in the king-post roof, the early 16th century font cover with folding back doors with linenfold, A helm over the door and a tablet to Thomas Sackville, d1692.

SELMESTON   *Dedication Unknown*   TQ 510070

The oldest features are a small lancet re-used in the east wall of the vestry on the south side and the blocked 14th century west doorway. The oak piers of the 14th century south arcade were renewed when the aisle was rebuilt in 1867. There is a 16th century Easter Sepulchre recess in the chancel. A bell-turret with a broach-spire rises from the nave roof.

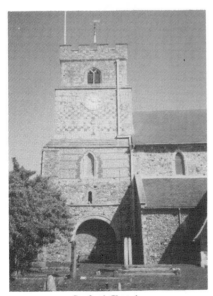

Seaford Church

Selmeston Church

Southease Church

SOUTHEASE   *Dedication Unknown*   TQ 423054

The church is now reduced to a Norman nave with a north doorway and one original window, plus a round west tower with original windows and a shingled conical roof. Nothing remains of the original square chancel, and only blocked arches remain of former chapels or short aisles flanking the east part of the nave. These parts may have gone as early as the 14th century, and a timber arch now divides off the nave east end as a chancel. There are Jacobean box-pews. On the north wall are faint remains of 13th century wall-paintings showing Christ's entry into Jerusalem, St Christopher, Christ before Pilate, Christ being scourged and the Crucifixion.

SOUTH MALLING   *St Michael*   TQ 413110

Over the porch outer entrance is the date 1628. The single body nave and chancel are of that period, the young John Evelyn having laid a foundation stone two years earlier, but the pyramidal-roofed west tower has 14th century features.

STANMER   *Dedication Unknown*   TQ 337097

Within the cruciform church of 1838 with a thin west tower lying by the University of Sussex are small figures of Sir John Pelham, d1580, and his wife and son, d1584 transferred here from the church of Holy Trinity at Minories in London.

STREAT   *Dedication Unknown*   TQ 351153

The nave masonry is Norman and the chancel is partly 13th century, when the nave west wall was thickened internally, perhaps to help carry the shingled bell-turret. The south aisle and all the other features are of the restoration of 1854. There are marble tablets with cherubs to William Bobell, d1752 and Mary Dobell, d1764. Of the same period are cast-iron slabs to members of the Gott and Saunders families.

TARRING NEVILLE   *St Mary*   TQ 444038

The chancel has 13th century lancets and the nave and south aisle under one roof are divided by a two bay arcade of the same period with double-chamfered arches and a round pier. The short west tower is rendered and pyramidal roofed. It too could be 13th century.

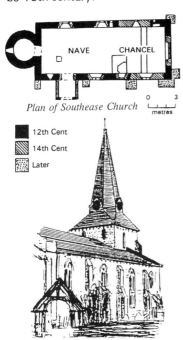

Plan of Southease Church

0   3
metres

■ 12th Cent
▨ 14th Cent
▦ Later

Uckfield Church

Old print of Udimore Church

Telscombe Church

TELSCOMBE   *St Lawrence*   TQ 405034

In the 1180s a three bay north chapel and a slightly wider two bay north chapel were added to the Norman nave and chancel. One respond of the chapel arcade has a multi-scalloped capital, the other crocket-leaves, the arches being round and unmoulded, like those of the aisle. The tower has a pointed unmoulded tower arch and lancet windows with round internal arches, so it is perhaps of c1200. Medieval stall ends have been re-used in the reading desk. The lectern also has old parts.

Ticehurst Church

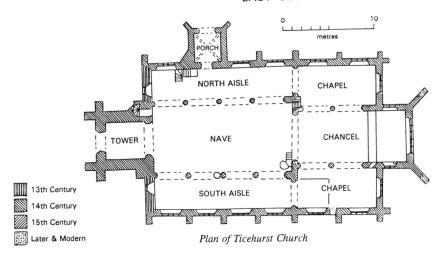

Plan of Ticehurst Church

13th Century
14th Century
15th Century
Later & Modern

TICEHURST   *St Mary*   TQ 689301

The positions of the 13th century west lancets indicate the aisles were originally narrower. Otherwise the church seems to be a complete 14th century rebuilding with a west tower with a big west doorway, corner buttresses and an embattled stair turret and short broach spire, and a chancel of three bays flanked by two bay chapels with their outer walls flush with those of the aisles. The renewed windows are of three lights with segmental arches except for the five light east window of 1856. The clerestory windows date from the same restoration by Slater. A 13th century arch is reused as the outer entrance to the vaulted north porch with an upper room. The arcades are of four bays with double-chamfered arches on octagonal piers. The 16th century octagonal font cover has doors that fold back and Flamboyant tracery panels. The chancel north window and the north aisle NW window have original stained glass. A late 14th century brass of a knight was later appropriated for John Wybarne, d1490 and is flanked by shorter figures of his wives. There is a cast-iron slab in the south chapel and there is a cartouche by Green to George Courthope, d1714.

UCKFIELD   *Holy Cross*   TQ 472214

The chancel and tower have masonry older than the rebuilding of 1839 by William Moseley but no medieval features survive apart from part of a 15th century font. The monuments include a brass of 1610, an iron slab of 1707 with an inscription across it, and a tablet to John Egles, d1750.

UDIMORE   *St Mary*   TQ 864189

The Norman nave has one blocked original window high up on the north. The two blocked doorways suggest a later lengthening and the blocked 13th century south arcade with double-chamfered arches also shows evidence of the third bay at the west end being later. Also 13th century are the short west tower with a pyramidal roof and rectangular SE stair-turret, and the chancel with single lancets along the sides and a widely spaced and stepped group of three in the east wall. The SW lancet has a blocked low-side window below it. One south window contains fragments of old glass and there is a spiral fluted shaft probably from a Norman pillar piscina.

WADHURST   *St Peter and St Paul*   TQ 641319

The west tower has two Norman windows, that at the bell-stage being of two lights. The broached and shingled needle spire may be 15th century, the age of the tower arch, the stair turret and the buttresses. The west doorway looks 15th century but is dated 1812. Both the nave and the 14th century chancel with some of the windows shafted inside are of a generous width. There are 13th century arcades of four bays with the central piers round and the others octagonal. The south aisle was widened in the 14th century and was given a new east window and a rib-vaulted porch with a room above in the 15th century. The north aisle keeps its 13th century width but was given 14th century windows and the east bay then expanded into a transept, east of which are modern vestries. The nave roof is 15th century whilst that in the south aisle is dated 1592. A font has been formed from a 13th century capital put on a base of that period. The many monuments include tablets to Mary Dunmoll, d1691, John Barham, 1730, several memorials to the Luck family in the porch, and a series of thirty cast-iron floor slabs, the earliest featuring shields and initials.

WALDRON   *All Saints*   TQ 549193

The 13th century chancel has a lancet in the north wall and two, now blocked, of what was perhaps a group of five in the east wall. The aisle is also 13th century, and wide for its period. The west tower is 15th century and has a higher NE stair-turret. The south aisle was added in 1859-62 by R.C.Hussey and the chancel south wall was then rebuilt. An old font lies outside by the porch. There is a monument to Major John Fuller, d1722. There is a tablet to Sir Thomas Dyke, d1706, and there are two other 18th century tablets, plus inscriptions to other members of the Dyke family.

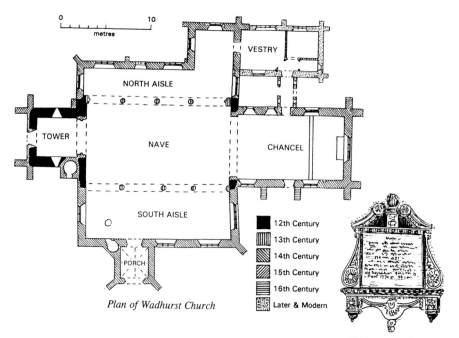

0		10
	metres	

VESTRY

NORTH AISLE

TOWER

NAVE

CHANCEL

SOUTH AISLE

PORCH

■ 12th Century
▦ 13th Century
▨ 14th Century
▧ 15th Century
▤ 16th Century
▦ Later & Modern

Plan of Wadhurst Church

Tablet at Wadhurst

Waldron Church

WARBLETON   *St Mary*   TQ 609182

The font and the chancel with lancets are 13th century. The segmental-arched south windows and the north aisle are 14th century but the arcade of four bays is 15th century, as is the west tower with heads projecting at the top. In the middle of the aisle is a squire's pew set on posts. Two windows contain fragments of old glass. There is a brass depicting William Prestwick, Dean of the college of St Mary at Hastings, d1436, under an ogival canopy. There is a cartouche of 1688 and a fine marble monument with a bust of Sir John Lade, d1740.

WARTLING   *St Mary Magdalene*   TQ 658092

The nave and chancel both have some 13th century masonry but the west wall is 14th century and the east wall is Victorian. There is a weatherboarded bell-turret over the nave west end. There are aisles of differing lengths flanking the eastern part of the nave. The two bay arcades are not in line with each other. The north aisle is 14th century but one window is 16th century. The south aisle is 15th century and has the Pelham buckle badge upon it. It and the chancel each have a blocked arch to a former south chapel probably demolished after the Reformation. There are box pews, a plain 18th century font and several Late Georgian tablets to the Curteis family.

WEST BLATCHINGTON   *St Peter*   TQ 280068

Only the south wall now remains of the Norman nave, west of which there was once an annex of uncertain date and purpose. The only ancient feature is the 15th century south doorway. By 1596 the church served only as a manorial chapel and was rarely used. It was a ruin from c1720 until 1890 when the late medieval chancel was entirely rebuilt and a vestry erected on the side of a south chapel. These parts now form a south aisle to a large new chamber built on the north side in the 1960s.

Westdean Church

Westfield Church

WESTDEAN   *All Saints*   TV 526997

The Norman nave has one original window on the north side and a blocked late 13th century window further east. The small lancet on the north suggests that the chancel the same width as the nave and undivided from it was built c1200, probably to replace an apse. Also the same width is the oblong west tower with a half-hipped spire. The tower has mostly 14th century features although the arch dividing it from the nave is older or is made up of older parts. Also 14th century are the south doorway and porch and a shafted tomb recess in the chancel north wall. A second tomb recess further west is late 13th century. Other monuments of note include those to William Thomas, d1639 and Susanna Tirrey, d1637.

Westham Church

WESTFIELD   *St John the Baptist*   TQ 810152

The Norman nave and chancel are connected by a narrow arch with one order of shafts. The chancel has one original window plus others of the 13th century. The south doorway and porch are 14th century but the door itself is dated 1542. The Norman west tower has big later clasping buttresses, one of which has a date plate of 1624, the probable age of the other buttresses and the remodelling of the nave Norman windows. The north aisle is an addition of 1860, and there is also a Victorian NW vestry. The square Jacobean pulpit has an 18th century tester with an inlaid star.

WEST FIRLE   *St Peter*   TQ 471072

The oldest feature is the reset round arched north doorway of c1200. The 13th century chancel has been much restored but retains a piscina and two lancets on the south side. Also 13th century are the west tower with heavy later corner buttresses and the reset south doorway. The arcades of four bays, the clerestory of cinquefoiled windows, the south aisle east window with original glass, and the window reset in the east wall of the 16th century north chapel are 14th century. The aisle outer walls and the south porch are 15th century. The chapel contains three tomb chests to members of the Gage family of Firle Place all made in 1595. One has effigies of Sir John, d1557 and his wife, and the others have brasses of Sir Edward, d1569 and John, d1595, and their wives. There are other brasses elsewhere in the church to Bartholomew Bolne, d1476 and his wife, and Thomas Gage, d1590, and his wife.

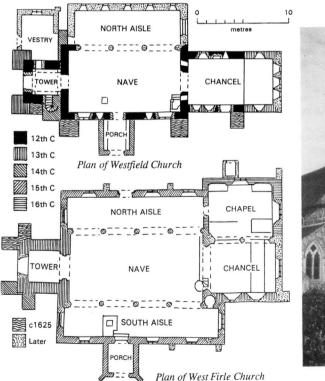

Plan of Westfield Church

Plan of West Firle Church

Tower at West Firle

Westmeston Church

WESTHAM   *St Mary*   TQ 642046

This church lies not far west of the west gate of the Roman fort at Pevensey and originally served a hospital of St Cross. This explains the Norman cruciform plan with a nave with three south windows above a string course and transepts with arches to former apses in their east walls. The south transept now has a hipped roof. The chancel is later, probably replacing a central apse, and there is a north aisle with a 14th century arcade with double-hollow-chamfered arches on octagonal piers. Of the 15th century are the north windows, the embattled diagonally-buttressed west tower, the screens dividing off the chancel and south transept, and fragments of stained glass figures in the east window.

WESTMESTON   *St Martin*   TQ 339137

The nave is Norman and has a north doorway, a tub font, and a chancel arch of that period. A new chancel was built in the 13th century, the piscina being of that period. The 14th century saw the nave given a new north window and a west doorway, and a south aisle added with a two bay arcade, whilst a south chapel was added c1500. The east wall has been entirely rebuilt and the rest much restored. Norman wall paintings of interest were then discovered but have not been preserved.

Whatlington Church

Brass at West Firle

WHATLINGTON   *St Mary Magdalene*   TQ 761182

The small 13th century nave and narrower chancel are covered by a continuous roof. There are clasping west buttresses. On the north side, towards the approach, are a porch-tower with a broach-spire and an apsidal vestry added in 1862 by S.W.Tracey.

WILLINGDON   *St Mary*   TQ 589025

The 13th century tower has a later shingled broach-spire. The nave of that period lay east of it but a new nave was built in the early 14th century and with the demolition of the old nave the two parts are now only joined at one corner. The new nave has square-headed windows with ogival-headed lights, a south doorway which is older work reset, and a king-post roof. The north arcade is also early 14th century. The series of monuments to the Parkers of Ratton starts with a small kneeling figure of Elinar, d1598. There are kneeling figures of Sir John, d1617, and his wife, and a recumbent effigy of Sir Nicholas, d1619, with kneeling children. The monument to Thomas, d1663, was made about fifty years later. There is a tablet to Sir George, d1726, and also cartouches to William Parker, d1700, and Katherine Nutt, d1727.

WILMINGTON   *St Mary and St Peter*   TQ 544043

The Norman chancel has two original windows and part of a triangle frieze, but the diagonally buttressed east wall is 15th century. Much of the nave, including the north doorway, is 14th century, but part of the north wall is also Norman, whilst the north transept now serving as a vestry with an organ blocking it off is 13th century. The two bay south arcade is 13th or 14th century but the aisle, which only flanked the nave east half, has been rebuilt, as has the chancel arch and the outer arch of the 15th century north porch. In the chancel is a small seated 13th century figure. The pulpit and tester are Jacobean. There is an Elizabethan monument in the south aisle. The church served a small Benedictine priory lying to the north.

Willingdon Church

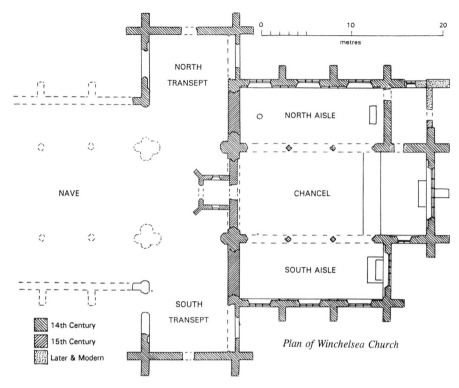

Plan of Winchelsea Church

NORTH TRANSEPT

NORTH AISLE

NAVE

CHANCEL

SOUTH AISLE

SOUTH TRANSEPT

14th Century
15th Century
Later & Modern

0   10   20
metres

WINCHELSEA   *St Thomas*   TQ 589025

Winchelsea was founded in 1283 by Edward I to replace an older settlement further east. It was intended to have three churches, St Thomas and St Giles, successors of churches in the old town, and a new foundation of St Leonard. Nothing remains of St Giles or St Leonard and St Thomas is only a fragment of what would have been one of England's grandest parish churches. The part currently in use is a wide chancel of c1300-20 four bays long set over a vaulted undercroft of two bays and with three of the bays flanked by wide chapels. East of the north chapel is a vestry. The windows are marble shafted (one contains old glass) and the piers have four main shafts and four marble subsidiary shafts. The roofs are single-framed with tie-beams. Ogees only occur in the sedilia and piscina of the south chapel, which must be a decade later than those of the chancel, and on the tombs. At the west end are three huge blocked arches which led into a crossing flanked by transepts of which the ruined end walls survive. There is doubt as to whether the nave and its aisles, which stopped one bay short of the west end, were ever completed. They may have been damaged by French raids in 1337 and 1380 and had gone by the end of the medieval period when a west porch was added where the crossing had been. A detached tower of stone and wood which lay in the churchyard was removed in 1790. In the south chapel are grand tombs of what are thought to be Gervase de Alard, d1310, first Admiral of the Cinque Ports, and a later Admiral, Stephen Alard, d1330, who founded a chantry in the church in 1312. The former monument has a Green Man upon the canopy. In the north chapel are three more effigies of a knight, a lady and a civilian. In the chancel floor is a brass of c1440 showing a civilian.

Winchelsea Church

WITHYHAM   *St Michael*   TQ 494356

Much of the church dates from between 1663, when it was struck by lightning, and 1672, the date of a sundial reset on the porch, although work on the large Sackville Chapel north of the chancel continued until 1680. The east windows of the chancel and chapel are typical debased late Gothic of the 17th century, that in the chancel having a transom. The embattled west tower is 14th century and the chancel has one south window of that period. The ridge of the nave roof lies much further north than that of the chancel, an odd effect resulting from rebuilding in the 1840s when the north arcade was removed but low south aisle added on, together with a porch. The octagonal font is of 1666. The Sackville Chapel contains a very fine monument with a reclining effigy of Thomas Sackville, d1677, aged thirteen, plus monuments to several later members of the family, by then Dukes of Dorset.

Withyham Church

OTHER ANGLICAN CHURCHES IN EAST SUSSEX

ASHURSTWOOD - Christ Church - 1884 by Lacy W.Ridge. 16th c. Flemish altarpiece
BEXHILL - All Saints - 1909 by Streatfield. Chancel & tower 1927-9.
BEXHILL - St Augustine - 1934 by W.H.Randoll Blacking. Completed 1960-3.
BEXHILL - St Barnabas - 1891 by Sir Arthur Blomfield. Aisles 1908-9. Chapel 1939.
BEXHILL - St Mark - Nave 1842, chancel & south aisle 1857, north aisle 1962.
BEXHILL - St Michael - 1929 by John B.Mendham. Brick. SW porch-tower.
BEXHILL - St Stephen - 1898-1900 by Henry Ward. Brick. East apse. SW tower.
BLACKHAM - All Saints - 1902 by L.W.Ridge. Small. Polygonal belfry on buttress.
BRIGHTON - All Souls - 1834. Classical. Chancel and nave roof with dormers 1879.
BRIGHTON - Annunciation - 1864. Wooden piers. Fine Morris & Burne-Jones window.
BRIGHTON - Christ Church - 1837-8 by George Cheeseman. Interior & roof of 1886.
BRIGHTON - Good Shepherd - 1921-2 by E.P. Warren. East end 1927. Brick.
BRIGHTON - St Bartholomew - 1872-4 by Edmund Scott. Brick. Very high & wide.
BRIGHTON - St George - 1824-5 by C.A.Busby. Yellow brick, windows in two tiers.
BRIGHTON - St John the Evangelist - 1840 by George Cheeseman. Classical style.
BRIGHTON - St John & St Peter - 1902 by Sir Arthur Blomfield. At Preston.
BRIGHTON - St Luke - 1881-5 by Sir Arthur Blomfield. Intended SW tower not built.
BRIGHTON - St Luke - 1875 by John Hill. Of little interest.
BRIGHTON - St Mark - 1840. South side later. West tower with recessed spire.
BRIGHTON - St Mary & St James - 1877-9, Sir William Emerson. NW tower not built.
BRIGHTON - St Matthew - 1881-3 by John Norton. Flint faced concrete.
BRIGHTON - St Michael - south side 1858-61, rest 1893, a fine design by Burges.
BRIGHTON - St Paul - 1846-8 by R.C.Carpenter for Rev H.M.Wagner. Older retable.
BRIGHTON - St Peter - 1824-8 by Sir Charles Barry. New chancel added 1900-6.
BRIGHTON - St Saviour - 1886 by Scott & Cawthorn. Flint & brick. At Preston.
BRIGHTON - St Wilfred - 1933-4 by H.S.Goodhart-Rendel. Tower over chancel.
BURWASH COMMON - St Philip - 1867 by Slater & Carpenter. Polygonal apse.
CAMBER - St Thomas - 1955-6, replacing a church destroyed in 1944.
CHAILEY - St Mary - 1876 by J.Oldrid Scott. Low central tower.
COLEMAN'S HATCH - Holy Trinity - 1913 by Sir Arthur Blomfield. SW tower & spire.
CRAWLEY DOWN - All Saints - 1843. East end, north aisle 1871. South aisle 1888.
CROSS-IN-HAND - St Bartholomew - 1864 by St Aubyn. Diagonal bell-turret.
DANEHILL - All Saints - 1892 by Bodley & Garner. Decorated style.
EASTBOURNE - All Saints - 1878-80 by T.E.C.Streatfield.
EASTBOURNE - Christ Church - 1859 by B.Ferrey, chancel 1879 by Scott & Hyde.
EASTBOURNE - Holy Trinity - 1837-9, Decimus Burton. Aisles 1855, east end 1861.
EASTBOURNE - St John - Tower 1868. New Church nearby 1955-7.
EASTBOURNE - St Michael - 1910-11 by G.E.S.Streatfield. Large, with west tower.
EASTBOURNE - St Peter - 1894-6 by H.Currey. Lancets.
EASTBOURNE - St Philip - 1903 by G.E.Powell. Red & Yellow brick. Lancets.
EASTBOURNE - St Saviour - 1867-8 by G.E.Street. NW tower. Brick.
ERIDGE - Holy Trinity - 1852-6. Turret over entrance. Straight-headed windows.
FAIRLIGHT - St Andrew - 1845 by T.Little. Lofty NW tower with turret.
FAIRWARP - Christ Church - 1881 by Rhode Hawkins. Enlarged 1930.
FALMER - St Lawrence - 1815 but made Neo-Norman in the 1850s.
FLIMWELL - St Augustine - 1839 by Decimus Burton. Chancel 1879.
FOREST ROW - Holy Trinity - 1836 by William Moseley. South aisle 1877-8.
FOREST ROW - St Richard de Wych - 1886. Apse, tower over vaulted crossing.
HADLOW DOWN - St Mark - 1836, rebuilt 1913 by G.Fellowes Prynne.
HAMMERWOOD - St Stephen - 1879-80 by E.P.Loftus Brock. SE tower & spire.
HASTINGS - All Souls - 1890 by Sir Arthur Blomfield. Brick, large, lancets.
HASTINGS - Christ Church - 18718-91 by R.H.Carpenter. Chancel decor 1899.
HASTINGS - Christ Church - 1878-81 by Gough. Small, SW turret. Old London Rd.

HASTINGS - Holy Trinity - 1851-9 by Teulon. tower over SW porch not built.
HASTINGS - St Andrew - 1869 by Habershon & Brock. Apse. Thin SE tower & spire.
HASTINGS - St Clement - 1838 by Thomas Catley. Lancets. Chancel added 1888.
HASTINGS - St Ethelburga - 1929 by J.B.Mendham.
HASTINGS - St John - SW tower 1881. Rest 1951 after wartime bombing.
HASTINGS - St Mary-in-the-Castle - 1828 by Joseph Kay.
HASTINGS - St Mary Magdalene - 1852 by Marrable. enlarged 1872. Tall SW tower.
HASTINGS - St Matthew - 1884 by Pearson. Transepts, apse, fleche. Brick.
HASTINGS - St Peter - 1885 by James Brooks. Polygonal NW baptistry.
HASTINGS - St Thomas of Canterbury - 1889 by C.A.Buckler.
HAYWARDS HEATH - St Wilfred 1863-5 by Bodley. Oblong central tower.
HIGH HURSTWOOD - Holy Trinity - 1870-2. South tower with timber top 1903.
HOLTYE COMMON - St Peter - 1892 by Lacy W.Ridge. Flying buttresses on west.
HORAM - Christ Church - 1890 by Percy Monkton.
HURST GREEN - Holy Trinity - 1884 by L.W.Ridge. Red brick. Two tier bellcote.
HOVE - All Saints - 1890-1 by Pearson. SW tower left incomplete.
HOVE - Bishop Hannington Memorial Church - 1938 by Sir Edward Maufe.
HOVE - Holy Trinity - 1862-4 by James Woodman. Apse. South porch-tower.
HOVE - St Andrew - 1827-8 by Barry. Italian Renaissance style. Chancel 1882.
HOVE - St Barnabas - 1882-3 by J. Pearson. Polygonal apse, transepts, fleche.
HOVE - St Patrick - 1858 by H.G.Kendall. Dormer clerestory windows. Rock-faced.
HOVE - St Thomas - 1913 by Claydon & Black. Red brick. Passage aisles.
LANGNEY - St Richard - 1956-8 by H.Hubbard Ford.
NETHERFIELD - St John Baptist - 1859 by S.S.Teulon. South tower. Bar-tracery.
NEW GROOMBRIDGE- St Thomas - 1883 by Norman Shaw. Perp style. West porch.
NEWHAVEN - Christ Church - 1881 by E.P.Loftus Brock. Red & yellow bricks.
NUTLEY - St James - 1845 by R.C.Carpenter, north aisle 1871.
OFFHAM - St Peter - 1859 by Ewan Christian. Apse, tower over chancel.
PLUMPTON GREEN - All Saints - 1893 by Samuel Denman. Octagonal tower.
POLEGATE - St John - 1874-6 by R.K.Blessley. Low NW tower with spire.
RYE HARBOUR - Holy Spirit - 1848-9 by S.S.Teulon. Enlarged in 1912.
ST LEONARDS - Christ Church - 1875 by Sir Arthur Blomfield. NW tower.
ST LEONARDS - St Leonard - 1953-61 by Sir Giles & Adrian Gilbert Scott.
ST LEONARDS - St Paul - 1868 by John Newton. NE tower by apse. Plate-tracery.
SAYERS COMMON - Christ Church - 1880 by Banks & Barry. 16th century glass.
SCAYNES HILL - St Augustine - 1858 by Habershon. Thin west tower. Brick.
SPITHURST - St Bartholomew - 1879-80 by Henry Card. Plate tracery & lancets.
STONE CROSS - St Luke - 1924. Brick, wooden windows. Central tower.
STONEGATE - St Peter - 1904 by Grenville Streatfeild. North tower with spire.
TIDEBROOK - St John Baptist - 1856 by Rushforth. Undercroft at west end.
TURNERS HILL - St Leonard - 1895 by Lacy Ridge. Tower & porches 1923 by Webb.
UPPER DICKER - Holy Trinity - 1843 by W.J.Donithorne. Neo-Norman. Font of 1663
WEST BLATCHINGTON - St Peter - Additions 1961 to church of 1890.
WITHYHAM - St John - 1839 by W.L.Blaker. Apsidal chancel added 1870.

GAZETTEER OF CHURCHES IN WEST SUSSEX

ALBOURNE   *St Bartholomew*   TQ 256162

The nave and north aisle date from a rebuilding by Scott in 1859 but the chancel has one Norman south window and a recess has imposts of an arch which probably led to an apse. The chevrons on the chancel arch are copied from original parts.

ALDINGBOURNE   *St Mary*   SU 923055

Of the early 12th century are a blocked window on the south, the west wall and the blocked three bay arcade of a former north aisle. The south aisle is probably of c1200, having a five bay arcade of pointed arches on round piers with scalloped capitals and a round-arched doorway with roll-mouldings and a label with dog-tooth ornament. The east bay is rib-vaulted. Of the 13th century are the west doorway with heads as hood-mould stops, the north transeptal tower, and the chancel with twin sedilia. Most of the windows are of Ewan Christian's restoration of 1867. The font with corner shafts and arcading is of c1200, and there are Royal Arms of William III.

AMBERLEY   *St Michael*   TQ 028132

The church lies immediately east of the castle of the Bishops of Chichester and its late 13th century tower overlooks the curtain wall. Looking into this tower is the west window of the impressive Norman nave. Two other large windows set in outer arches and a blocked doorway remain in the north wall and there is an impressive chancel arch of three orders with chevrons, the triple responds having shafts with volute capitals. In 1230s Bishop Ralph Neville, then Chancellor, rebuilt the chancel with three bays of side lancets and a group of three in an east wall with clasping angle-buttresses. The south aisle with a three bay arcade is also 13th century but the south doorway cannot be earlier than c1300. There is a Norman font with four blank arches on each side. On the south side of the chancel arch a wall painting of a Crucifixion has been revealed. There is a brass to John Wantele, d1424.

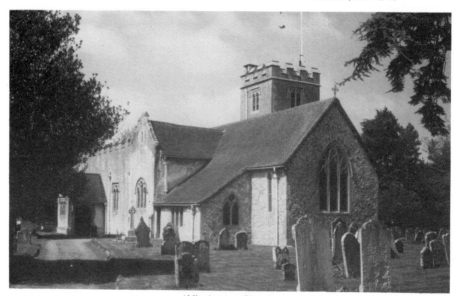

Aldingbourne Church

Amberley Church

ANGMERING *St Margaret* TQ 067044

The diagonally buttressed west tower with a battlements and a higher NE stair-turret was built in 1507 at the expense of Syon Abbey in Middlesex. The rest of the church was mostly rebuilt in 1852-3 by S.S.Teulon except for the chancel arch of c1200, the arch to the Gratwick Chapel on the south side, and the moved south doorway.

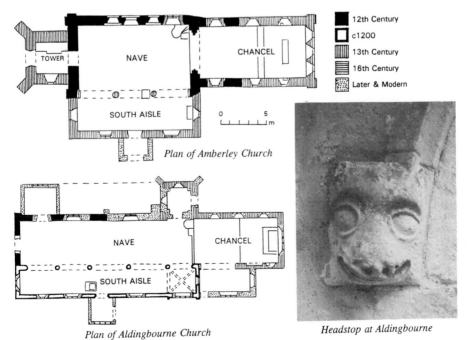

Plan legend:
- 12th Century
- c1200
- 13th Century
- 16th Century
- Later & Modern

Plan of Amberley Church

Plan of Aldingbourne Church

Headstop at Aldingbourne

Ardingley Church

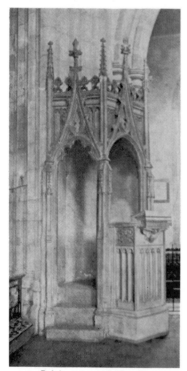

Pulpit at Arundel Church

APULDRAM   *St Mary*   SU 842034

A long path leads to the church, which was a chapel-of-ease to Bosham. It is a 13th century building of nave, south aisle with a three bay arcade of double-chamfered arches, and a chancel with groups of three lancets with shafts and arcading not only in the east wall, as is common, but in the north and south walls as well. The bell-turret dates from the restoration of 1877 by Lacy W.Ridge. Of the 14th century are the screen in the aisle and tiles on the altar-step.

ARDINGLEY   *St Peter*   TQ 339299

The oldest relic is a loose Norman scalloped capital. The south arcade of two wide bays is 14th century but the responds with angle shafts look like 13th century work. Also 14th century are the chancel and the lower part of the tower, which has a 16th or 17th century top. The north aisle is of 1887 by Carpenter and Ingelow. There is a late medieval screen. The altar rail with twisted balusters is of c1700. The monuments include a damaged effigy of a priest of c1330, brasses depicting Richard Wakeherst, d1455, and his wife under canopies, and brasses of Richard Culpeper and his wife, d1504, and Nicholas Culpeper, d1510, and his wife, a Wakehurst.

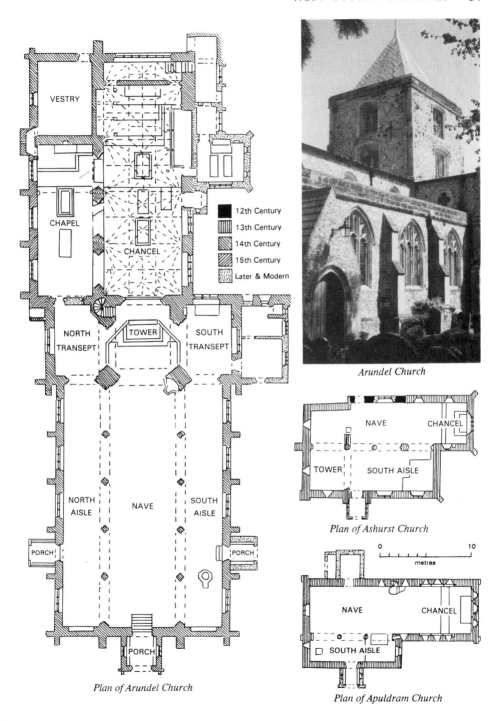

VESTRY

CHAPEL

CHANCEL

	12th Century
	13th Century
	14th Century
	15th Century
	Later & Modern

NORTH TRANSEPT

TOWER

SOUTH TRANSEPT

NORTH AISLE

NAVE

SOUTH AISLE

PORCH

PORCH

PORCH

Plan of Arundel Church

Arundel Church

NAVE

CHANCEL

TOWER

SOUTH AISLE

Plan of Ashurst Church

0   10
metres

NAVE

CHANCEL

SOUTH AISLE

Plan of Apuldram Church

ARUNDEL   *St Nicholas*   TQ 016073

Except for the 15th century Lady Chapel and the Victorian south porch the church is entirely of the twenty years after 1380 when it was made collegiate. It has a central tower with two tiers of low bell openings and transepts projecting only slightly further than the aisles of the nave. The arcade piers of the five bay arcades have four shafts and four hollows and octagonal abaci and the arches have double-hollow-chamfers. There is a stone west porch. The chancel is four bays long and has a vault of 1886 incorporating medieval bosses from the original vault taken down in 1782. This part is now called the Fitzalan Chapel and has long been closed off from the rest of the church by a screen. This part is still a Catholic chapel and is only reached through the grounds of the castle, then into the original sacristy on the north side, and then through into the Lady Chapel flanking the remainder of this side. The Fitzalan Chapel has four-light windows with tiers of quatrefoils in the tracery.

The octagonal font has pairs of trefoil-headed panels. It is also late 14th century, as is the pulpit, although the latter has been remodelled. The Lady Chapel contains medieval stalls with faces and one misericord. In the Fitzalan chapel is a life size Crucifixus probably made in Spain in the 15th century. The collection of brasses includes two 15th century priests, one a half figure, canopied figures of Thomas Salmon, d1430 and his wife, d1418, and others of John Threel, d1465, Robart Ward, d1474, John Baker, d1456, and Esperaunce Blondell.

The tombs of the Fitzalan Earls of Arundel in the Fitzalan Chapel and Lady Chapel form one of the finest collections of funerary monuments to be seen in a British parochial or collegiate church. There are recumbent effigies of Thomas, 5th Earl, d1415, and his wife, d1439. John, 6th Earl, d1421, has a tomb chest without an effigy. John, 7th Earl, killed leading an English army at Beauvais in 1435, has both an effigy and a cadaver above. Against the south wall is the chantry with twisted shafts and tomb of William, 9th Earl, d1487, and his wife, d1462. There is a triple tomb to the 10th, 11th, and 12th earls, d1524, 1544 and 1580, although the latter has another monument as well. There is also a monument to Robert Spyller, d1633, plus tombs and effigies of several 19th century Dukes of Norfolk.

Fitzalan Chapel at Arundel Church

ASHINGTON   *St Peter and St Paul*   TQ 121159

The church was heavily restored and given a large new aisle in 1872 by Robert Wheeler. Some 15th century windows remain and a stoup reset in the aisle.

ASHURST   *St James*   TQ 176164

The nave north doorway and some walling is Norman. Three windows are of 1877, but the rest of the stonework (and the font) seems to be of c1200-20. It consists of a chancel the same width as the short nave, a wide south aisle with a two bay arcade and then another arch (probably slightly later) into the chancel, a tower west of the aisle, and a low west extension of the nave with a roof abutting against the tower. Thus both the layout and the elevations are quite unusual, but picturesque.

BALCOME   *St Mary*   TQ 308310

In 1847-50 a new nave with a north aisle was added on the north side of a small 13th century church of a low west tower with a broach-spire, nave and chancel.

BARGHAM   *Dedication Unknown*

In a remote position against the Downs are foundations excavated in the 1950s of a church demolished c1500. It was a Saxon building of nave and chancel with the very unusual feature of a west apse incorporating Roman brick fragments. Porticus were added later, and in the 12th century these and the chancel were given east apses, but the chancel was given a square end again in the 13th century.

BARLAVINGTON   *St Mary*   SU 978155

The chancel with two round-headed east lancets and the two bay arcades are of c1200. The north arcade is blocked. That on the south was opened out for a new aisle added in 1874. The arcades have round piers with square abaci.

BARNHAM   *St Mary*   SU 956036

This is a single chamber with a tympanum of wood and plaster instead of a chancel arch. Two Norman windows remain on the south side. There is a blocked north arcade of c1190 with crude pointed arches simply broken through the wall. Another arch of this date connects the chancel and vestry. The west window and doorway are 15th century and there is a white-painted wooden bell-turret. The 13th century chancel has a trefoil-headed piscina, windows on the south with a pair of lancets with a lozenge above (i.e crude plate tracery), and three lancets in the east wall. There is a fine 15th century painted wooden figure of St Genevieve made in France.

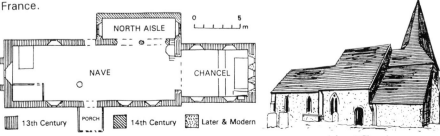

Plan of Chidham Church   *Ashurst Church*

BEPTON   *St Mary*   SU 855183

This church has been much rebuilt but original 13th century features are the fine crocketted tomb recess and cross-slab in the chancel, the nave south doorway and the pyramidal-roofed west tower with heavy 17th century diagonal buttresses.

BERSTED   *St Mary Magdalene*   SU 935002

The west tower of c1200 has large later buttresses. There are narrow aisles with five bay arcades of the mid 13th century with double-chamfered arches on piers alternately round and octagonal, but the outer walls and chancel are mostly of the restoration of 1879-81 by Wan Christian.

BIGNOR   *Holy Cross*   SU 982146

There is a wide Norman chancel arch but the other features are 13th century, the lancets being externally renewed in a restoration by Street, when the bell-turret was added and a new west window provided. The chancel has three east lancets and there are narrow aisles with arcades with double-chamfered arches. The much restored screen is 14th century. A porch lies to the west of the south aisle.

BILLINGSHURST   *St Mary*   TQ 088259

The large but low tower with a broach-spire has one 13th century lancet and several 16th century windows. In front of it is brick and timber porch of c1600. The east end dates from the restoration of 1866 but the south chapel retains 13th century work and the arcades of double-chamfered arches on octagonal piers are perhaps of c1300. There are 15th century windows in the south aisle and 16th century windows in the north aisle. The 15th century wagon roof has square panels with carved bosses at the beam intersections. There is a brass to Thomas Bartlet, d1499, and his wife.

BINSTED   *St Mary*   SU 982060

The nave and chancel are both Norman and only separated by timber framing similar to that supporting the shingled bell-turret. One of the three original windows has the embrasure painted with a contemporary picture of St Margaret and a Tree of Life, now very faded. The font with an arcaded bowl on a thick stem is Late Norman.

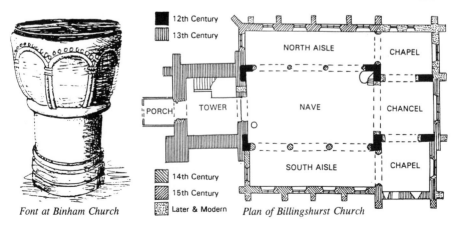

12th Century
13th Century
14th Century
15th Century
Later & Modern

NORTH AISLE   CHAPEL
PORCH   TOWER   NAVE   CHANCEL
SOUTH AISLE   CHAPEL

Font at Binham Church   *Plan of Billingshurst Church*

Billingshurst Church

Porch at Billingshurst Church

BIRDHAM   *St James*   SU 824003

This church was heavily restored in 1882 by G.M.Mills, when the chancel was rebuilt and one north window moved further east so that the organ would not block it. The 14th century nave retain original north and south doorways. The diagonally-buttressed west tower with a SE stair-turret dates from the 1540s, although the clustered shafts of the tower arch could possibly be 14th century.

BOLNEY   *St Mary Magdalene*   TQ 263228

Original features of the Norman nave and chancel are the south doorway with reeded bands around the arch and a hood-mould and two chancel windows. The chancel inclines to the north from the nave central axis. The east window with Y-tracery is of c1300. The west tower is known to be of the 1530s and has carved spandrels on the doorway typical of that date, although the conical pinnacles look later. The south porch is of 1718. The north aisle and vestry beyond to the NE are of 1853.

Binsted Church

BOSHAM   *Holy Trinity*   SU 804039

This church appears in a stylised form on the Bayeux Tapestry since Harold Godwinson sailed from here in 1064, ending up in the hands of Duke William of Normandy. Thus it comes as no surprise to find the church has a rectangular Saxon tower with a typical triangular-headed window over the tower arch and a blocked two-light window on the north side. The top stage and broach-spire are 15th century. Even more important Saxon work is the very fine chancel arch probably of the 1040s when Earl Godwin probably had his chief seat at Bosham. The arch is roll-moulded and stands on boldly shafted responds set on circular bases. The base of an arch of a Roman basilica is said to remain below it. The west bay of the chancel retains Saxon herringbone masonry with traces of a window on the north side. The second bay is Norman and the third bay is of c1230 with coupled lancets with Purbeck marble shafts on the sides and a set of five stepped lancets with shafts in the east wall. There is a double piscina on the south side. A 13th century vestry north of the chancel has been much altered.

The aisles are also 13th century with four bay arcades of double-chamfered arches on circular piers with spur bases, one of which has monster heads. The circular windows over the spandrels of the north arcade are probably contemporary with it rather than Saxon as has been claimed. The north aisle has a piscina which incorporates a Norman pillar piscina as its drain. In the 14th century the aisles were given new windows (those on the south are renewed) and that on the south gained a tomb recess, a new doorway, and a rib-vaulted crypt at the east end, half below the floor level and half above it. The octagonal font with four shafts and plain arcading is of c1200. One south window contains stained glass roundels of angels from Norwich Cathedral. In the chancel is a damaged effigy of a 15th century lady.

Interior of Bosham Church

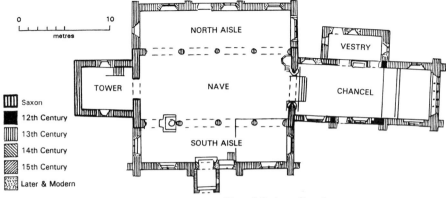

Saxon

12th Century

13th Century

14th Century

15th Century

Later & Modern

Plan of Bosham Church

BOTOLPHS   *St Botolph*   TQ 194093

The chancel is Late Saxon with one original window and a crudely roll-moulded chancel arch. A mid 13th century north aisle has gone but the three arches of the arcade remain in the north wall. Also 13th century is the pyramidal-roofed west tower. The east window is early 14th century. There are abstract patterns on the 17th century pulpit and tester. There are slight traces of medieval wall-paintings.

Blocked arcade at Botolphs Church

Interior of Boxgrove Priory Church

BOXGROVE   *St Mary and St Blaise*   SU 908075

The plain transepts and the entrance to the former chapter house beyond the north transept go back to shortly after a Benedictine priory was founded here c1117. East of it is the fine aisled choir of the 1220s eight bays long with a clerestory of lancets and vaulting throughout. The bays are narrow with sharply pointed arcade arches and the upper parts pair the bays together under round arches, this pattern also being reflected in the design of alternating piers. These have detached Purbeck marble shafts and there is much use of dog-tooth ornamentation on the arches. At the east end are three tall lancets. On the ceiling is a mid 16th century painting by Lambert Bernard with intertwined heraldry and foliage.

The crossing tower dates from the 1170s and about that time a new twelve bay aisled nave was laid out. In the 1220s it was vaulted in six bays in the same manner as the choir, but vaulting was evidently intended from the start. Because the cloister lay against part of the nave north wall only the western five bays on that side were aisled. A large south porch has vanished and only fragments remain of the ten western bays of the nave, since it was pulled down at the Dissolution, the choir being adequate for the parish. The pulpitum was incorporated in the wall blocking off the ruined part. South of the two surviving bays is a 14th century chamber and there are later medieval windows in the transepts, which were then given wooden galleries.

The octagonal font with shields in quatrefoils is 15th century. There are medieval tiles in the chancel south aisle. The church contains a number of late medieval tomb recesses and chests and one important monument, the luxuriously decorated chantry of Lord de la Warr, d1526, and his wife, d1532. This has a fan vault and mixes Gothic and Renaissance motifs quite freely. Other monuments include those of Sir William Morley, erected 1728, and Mary, Countess of Derby, d1752, erected c1770.

Bramber Church

BRAMBER   *St Nicholas*   TQ 186106

The church lies just below the entrance to William de Braose's castle and served it as a chapel. It has late 11th century herringbone masonry. The church was cruciform but is thought to have been damaged during the Civil War and is now reduced to the nave and a chancel created in the 19th century under the crossing tower. The arch between the two parts has very crudely carved capitals. The blocked arches to the transepts also remain, and a narrow blocked arch in the nave north wall which is harder to explain as it is too wide for a doorway. The church is now entered through a vestry-porch extension of 1931 at the west end. The Norman doorway with billets on the hood-mould in the nave SE corner may not be in its original position.

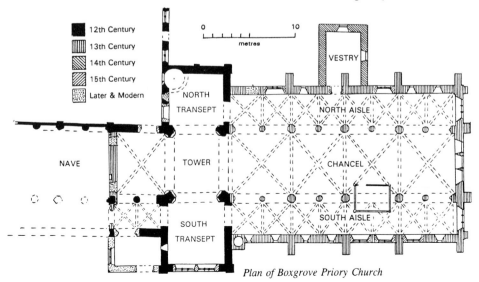

Plan of Boxgrove Priory Church

Broadwater Church

BROADWATER   *Dedication Unknown*   TQ 146044

By c1160 the church consisted of a nave, central tower and chancel. The east arch of the crossing has much chevron ornamentation and shows signs of sagging. The west arch was later made pointed when the nave was provided with aisles with four-bay arcades of double-chamfered arches on circular piers. In the 15th century piers were given new bases and capitals and the aisles and clerestory provided with segmental headed two-light windows. The west front is 19th century. The transepts are late 12th century and show signs of possibly having had two storeys, the lower stage with modest windows and the upper having an east doorway. Of the same period is the bell-stage of the central tower with two windows on each side (but three towards the east), round-headed but with pointed outer arches with nook-shafts. Also late 12th century is the chancel with a string-course of chevrons and pellets and a quadripartite vault. The east wall is entirely of 1857-66.

The chancel stalls feature misericords. In the chancel floor is a brass with a figure of a priest under a canopy of John Mapilton, d1432, rector and chancellor to Henry V's queen Joan of Navarre. In the chancel north wall is a tomb with a three-part canopy of Thomas, 5th Lord de la Warr. In the south transept is a monument with Renaissance detail to Thomas, 6th Lord de la Warr, d1554. It has figures of the Virgin and St George flanking a former Christ in Majesty.

BUNCTON   *All Saints*   TQ 145139

The nave and chancel of the small isolated church appear to be mostly Norman with tiny original windows high up. The chancel has 13th century lancets on the north and south and a piscina and east wall with buttresses and a two-light window of the 14th century. The outside of it has pointed arches with motifs such as beakheads and intersecting arches of the late 12th century. They have probably been imported from a monastic house after the Reformation. The interior is delightfully unrestored and the only obviously 19th century feature is the bellcote.

Detail of monument at Broadwater

Broadwater Church

BURPHAM   *St Mary*   TQ 039090

The nave north wall with a doorway and a blocked window is probably late 11th century and until 1800 there was a plain Early Norman chancel arch. The north transept is probably early 12th century whilst the south transept, although rebuilt along with the south aisle in 1869 by Sir T.G.Jackson, has a very fine arch of c1160 towards the nave with two orders with roll mouldings and chevrons. The two arches forming the south arcade are of the 1170s, while the chancel is probably of c1185-90. It has quadripartite vaulting and three modest east lancets. The vault is carried on corbels with scallops and waterleaf. Original are the piscina and double aumbry. There are also 14th century windows in the chancel, whilst the west tower and the octagonal font with rosettes in quatrefoils and a panelled stem are 15th century. The altar rail is early 17th century and there are three 17th to 18th century chandeliers.

Buncton Church   *Burpham Church*

BURTON   *Dedication Unknown*   SU 967175

The church lies by the house and is unrestored. The walls are Norman but the square-headed mullioned windows are the result of repairs ordered in 1636 by Archbishop Juxon. The delightful interior has a 15th century screen with an embattled rood beam below a plater tympanum with the Commandments, painted Royal Arms of Charles I dated 1636, and modern bench in which 16th century linenfold panels are re-used. There is a 15th century effigy of a lady in the chancel. There are small brasses of John Goring, d1521, and of the wife, d1558, of Sir William Goring, d1553.

BURY   *St John the Evangelist*   TQ 016131

The pointed and single chamfered tower arch is of c1200 but the tower itself may be two generations older, as may be the nave north wall. The south arcade is of about the same period, the arches having a chamfered inner order and a moulded outer order. The chancel arch is 14th century, the octagonal font with rosettes, the simple rood screen, and several of the windows are 15th century, and the south doorway and porch are early 16th century. The pulpit of 1628 has pokerwork patterns. In the 19th century the chancel was rebuilt and a south vestry added.

CHICHESTER   *All Saints in the Pallant*   SU 862046

This is a 13th century single chamber with a six lancets and blocked doorway in the south wall, five lancets on the north, and three renewed lancets with nook-shafts and moulded rere-arches in the east wall. The west doorway is 15th century. Apart from a NW buttress the only projection is a 19th century north vestry and organ chamber.

CHICHESTER   *St Andrew Oxmarket*   SU 862048

This church, now used for other purposes, is reached from the north side of East Street by an alleyway. It is a plain 13th century single chamber with a west doorway. The north and south walls each have a lancet at the east end, then a 14th century window, and a 15th century window further south, and there are traces of an original blocked south doorway. The 19th century restored the east window, added a north vestry and the west buttresses. Two 16th century monuments are built into the outside walls, whilst inside is a frontal bust of John Cawley, c1690.

CHICHESTER   *St Bartholomew*   SU 856048

A classical style church of 1832 by George Draper, with an chancel of 1929 stands on the site of a circular-naved church of St Sepulchre destroyed in 1642.

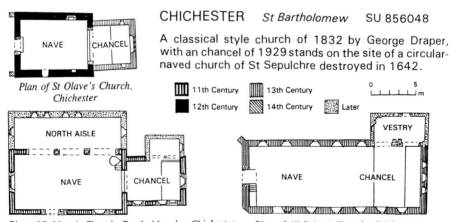

Plan of St Olave's Church, Chichester

11th Century   12th Century   13th Century   14th Century   Later

0   5 m

Plan of St Mary's Church, Rumboldswyke, Chichester   Plan of All Saints' Church, Chichester

All Saints' Church, Chichester

St Pancras' Church, Chichester

CHICHESTER   *Greyfriars*   SU 863051

Standing alone within Priory Park is the choir of a Franciscan friary begun as soon as the convent moved to this spot in 1269 and probably completed by 1282. Each of the five windows on each side has two pointed lights with a quatrefoil above, and the east wall has five tall stepped lancets under an outer arch, a conservative design for the date. The outer lights were shortened and given cusps when a new wagon roof was provided in the 15th century. The two blocked north doorways presumably led to a cloister. The chancel arch is blocked and there may never have been a nave. Inside are a plain piscina, sedilia, and a tomb recess.

CHICHESTER   *St Mary*   SU 894026

What was once the village church of Rumboldswyke SE of the city is now surrounded by suburbia. The nave and chancel are 11th century, with a plain round arch between them. The roll-moulded south doorway (with adjacent stoup) and renewed 13th century lancets make the building look Victorian but only the north aisle, the west window, and the small organ chamber beside the chancel are actually of that period.

CHICHESTER   *St Olave*   SU 861049

This church on the east side of North Street is now an S.P.C.K bookshop. It has a much restored tiny 13th century chancel set at an angle to a modest Norman nave, in which is reset a 14th century piscina with an ogival head. Also 14th century are the west doorway and window and the trefoiled lancets inn the chancel side walls. The chancel floor is paved with 15th and 17th century encaustic tiles.

CHICHESTER   *St Pancras*   SU 865048

This is a small Gothick church of 1750 by William Ride by Eastgate Square. It has a west tower, nave and chancel. The windows contain contemporary heraldic glass. The interior was remodelled in 1868 by G.M.Hills and a north aisle then added.

CHICHESTER   *St Peter the Great*   SU 858048

In the fine church of 1848-52 by R.C.Carpenter in West Street is an octagonal 15th century font with two trefoiled panels on each side, probably from the cathedral.

CHICHESTER   *St Peter the Less*   SU 860051

Nothing now remains of this church on the east side of North Street demolished in 1957. A wide 19th century chancel dwarfed a small 13th century nave with three north lancets, on the south side of which was a tiny 14th century aisle of just one bay with an equally tiny porch-tower at the west end of it.

CHIDHAM   *St Mary*   SU 787039

The long nave and the chancel are both 13th century with lancets, although the east end was been rebuilt during a restoration of 1864. A bellcote is supported on big clasping buttresses. There is a short 14th century north aisle with a two bay arcade and one original two-light window. A date of c1660 has been suggested for the font but it could be of almost any pre-Victorian period. In the chancel are cartouches to Henry Bickley, d1707, and George Meggott, d1708.

CHITHURST   *Dedication Unknown*   SU 843231

This is a little altered late 11th century church of nave and chancel with a narrow round arch between them and herringbone masonry and one tiny original window on the north side. Of the late 13th century are one cusped lancet and the two-light east window, and of the early 14th century are the west doorway and a south window.

Chithurst Church

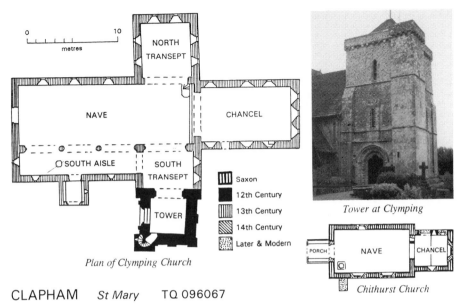

Tower at Clymping

Saxon
12th Century
13th Century
14th Century
Later & Modern

Plan of Clymping Church

Chithurst Church

CLAPHAM   *St Mary*   TQ 096067

The church is mostly 13th century with a chancel with lancets, a NW tower, a north arcade with foliage capitals on the piers and a south arcade of about a generation later. One Norman window can be traced over the north arcade. There are several 15th century two-light windows. Monuments to the Shelley family include several brasses, notably those depicting John, d1526, and his wife, and a tomb recess with kneeling effigies of Sir William, d1548, and his wife Alice with fourteen children.

CLYMPING   *St Mary*   TQ 004026

This is a fine cruciform church almost entirely of the 1220s. There are three lancets with shallow roll-mouldings in each side of the chancel and a more closely grouped set of three in the east wall, plus the usual piscina and aumbry with trefoiled heads, whilst the north transept has two lancets on each side. The nave has three lancet on the north and a three bay arcade to an aisle with a central porch on the south. The south transept is shorter than its counterpart and has beyond it a fine ashlar-faced tower which is of the 1180s below and the 1220s above. There are clasping corner buttresses, that at the SW enlarged to contain a stair, and mid-wall buttresses in which are pierced windows with chevrons almost obscuring a roll-moulding. One of these buttresses rises from the hoodmould with dogtooth of a splendid west facing doorway with chevrons and a trefoil-headed inner arch. Remarkably, there are no later alterations evident in the church. Later only are the late 13th century chest with pointed-trefoiled arcading, the plain bench ends with trefoil-headed lights flanked by buttresses, and the 15th century stone pulpit.

COATES   *St Agatha*   SU 998178

This is a tiny church in an isolated position. The nave and chancel are probably both Norman but there seems to have been much refacing outside and the bell-turret is of 1907. One small window remains on the south side but the other windows are 13th century enlargements. The north doorway and the priest's doorway are 15th century.

Tower at Coldwaltham

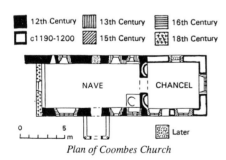

Plan of Coombes Church

Brass at Cowfold

COCKING   *Dedication Unknown*   SU 879175

The nave and chancel are both Norman and the original plain chancel arch survives along the tub font and parts of three windows, one of which (over the south arcade) has traces of a 13th century mural of the Angel appearing to the Shepherds. One chancel window is 13th century. Other chancel windows and the ogival-headed recess, the south aisle with a two bay arcade, and the angle-buttressed west tower are 14th century. The exterior looks Victorian as a result of refacing of the south aisle and chancel and the addition in 1865 of the north aisle.

Coombes Church

Wall painting at Coombes

COLDWALTHAM   *St Giles*   TQ 024166

The church was mostly rebuilt in 1871 except for the late 13th century south arcade and the tower of c1200 with lancets, very low clasping corner buttresses, and a half-timbered bell-stage of later date below the pyramidal roof.

COMPTON   *St Mary*   SU 777148

The chancel of c1200 has three small lancets and a plain pointed chancel arch with a single-chamfer. The blocked two bay north arcade with waterleaf on the pier capital is slightly earlier, whilst the three bay south arcade with double-chamfered arches and on round and one octagonal pier is a little later. In 1849 the aisle was rebuilt wider and one bay longer and the nave also rebuilt longer. It has a timber bell-turret with a shingled spire. There is a tablet with an urn to Sarah Phipps, d1793.

COOMBES   *Dedication Unknown*   TQ 191082

The nave is late 11th century and has fine set of wall-paintings of c1100, patterns and a dramatic weight-bearing figure even appearing on the soffit of the chancel arch, above which is Christ in Majesty, and, lower down, Christ delivering the keys to St Peter and the book to St Paul. The Visitation appears over the south doorway and a Nativity series on the north wall. The chancel of c1200 has 15th century windows either side of the original priest's doorway. The east window is 16th century whilst the west window is of 1724. There are mercifully no Victorian alterations.

COWFOLD   *St Peter*   TQ 213226

The glory of the church is the brass on the nave floor showing Thomas Nelond, 26th prior of Lewes, d1433, under a complex canopy with a surrounding inscription. The chancel has 13th century lancets on the north side, one of then having late medieval stained glass showing the Crucifixion. Others on the south side are now blocked. Money for building the south chapel was left in 1530. It has a four-centred arch towards the chancel. The four bay arcade is similar. Beside the Victorian chancel arch is a canopy in which stood an effigy of the Virgin. The font was purchased in 1481. The tower with a NW stair turret and angle buttresses is also of about that date.

CRAWLEY   *St John the Baptist*   TQ 268366

When the 15th century diagonally buttressed west tower was refaced in 1807 three frontal medieval figures were placed over the west window. The west doorway is original. The nave south wall may be 13th century and the roof with tie-beams and wind-braces is 15th century but the windows are of 1879-80, the date of the chancel, north aisle and north vestry. The pulpit was once dated 1627. The altar rail with twisted balusters is late 17th century. There is a brass of a female of c1510.

CUCKFIELD   *Holy Trinity*   TQ 303245

Three bays of the south arcade and the tower with a broach-spire recessed within battlements on a frieze of pointed trefoils are 13th century. In the early 14th century the tower was given diagonal buttresses and the arcade was given an extra bay, and a four bay north arcade was built with hexagonal piers, plus a new chancel and chapels with two-bay arcades. There are straight-headed windows with ogee-headed lights of this period. The quatrefoil clerestory was blocked after a new roof with tie-beams on traceried spandrels was provided in the late 15th century and were only revealed again in 1925. The Sergison Chapel, now a vestry, beyond the north chapel is 16th century. The church was restored by Bodley in 1855-6 and the south porch was added by his pupil C.E.Kempe in 1883, whilst R.H.Carpenter designed the north porch of 1878. The monuments include a brass to Henry Bowyer, d1589, a slate to Guy Carleton, d1628, a kneeling effigy of the young Ninian Burrell, d1628, and memorials to Charles Serison, d1732, and Sir William Burrell, d1797.

DIDLING   *St Andrew*   SU 835182

This tiny and remote-sited 13th century church consisted of a nave and chancel but in the 14th century the chancel was given a new south wall in line with that of the nave and the two parts then became a single chamber. The north lancets are original, the two east lancets and one west lancet were reset when those ends were rebuilt in brick c1800. The south windows are 14th century except for one of the 16th century, with which goes the north doorway. There are plain medieval pews with two knobs on the ends, a tub font which is probably older than the church, a Jacobean altar rail and Victorian oil lambs in the delightfully unrestored interior.

Plan of Didling Church

13th Century
14th Century
15th Century
16th Century
Later & Modern

Plan of Cuckfield Church

Donnington Church

Doorway at Crawley

DONNINGTON   *Holy Trinity*   SU 853022

In the 16th century a plain tower replaced the south aisle west bay as there was insufficient space beyond the west wall for a tower there. Otherwise, apart from the 19th century Trinity Chapel, this is an early 13th century building with arcades of four bays and a chancel with three lancets on each side, a trefoil-headed piscina, and a group of thee east lancets with continuously moulded rere-arches and a triple hood-mould. In 1939 a fire destroyed the old furnishings but there remain a monument to John Page, d1779, and two busts of the 1840s to members of the Crosbie family.

EARNLEY   *Dedication Unknown*   SZ 816968

Forming a single chamber are a 13th century nave with Victorian windows and porch but an original doorway and a 14th century chancel with a two light each window, ogee-headed single-light side windows, an aumbry and an ogee-headed piscina.

EARTHAM   *St Margaret*   SU 938093

The Norman nave has an original west doorway and a narrow chancel arch of two orders, the inner one resting on demi-shafts with volute capitals carved with a face and a rabbit. The openings on either side of the chancel arch are of 1869 when the chancel was rebuilt and a west porch added. The narrow 13th century south aisle has an arcade of two wide bays with double-chamfered arches. The aisle is lighted by just a tiny lancet at each end. There is a monument to Thomas Hayley, d1800.

Easebourne Church

Eastergate Church

EASEBOURNE   *St Mary*   SU 895225

This church served an Augustinian nunnery founded in the 1230s, parts of the claustral buildings of which are incorporated in a house to the south. The nuns took over an 11th century church of which the nave with herringbone masonry flanking a blocked doorway still survives in a much altered state. A late 12th century west tower, a square font with blind arcading, and the west arch of a three bay north arcade, also late 12th century, have survived the drastic restoration of the rest by A.W.Blomfield in 1876. The nuns built a wide new north aisle but of it little remains apart from a tomb recess now containing an effigy of Sir David Owen, d1535. This and several other monuments, including effigies of the first Viscount Montague, d1592, and his two wives, have been brought here from Midhurst.

EAST DEAN   *All Saints*   SU 905131

The transepts and central tower with two-light bell-openings are Norman. The south doorway of c1200 has two orders of roll-mouldings and columns. Of the 13th century are the chancel side walls and the west and north walls of the nave, with two blocked arches for a former arcade in the latter. The transepts were partly rebuilt later, c1300 on the north and c1340 on the south if the east windows are anything to go by. The chancel east wall and the crossing arches are Victorian. The octagonal Norman font has a base which looks like an upturned scalloped capital.

EASTERGATE   *St George*   SU 945051

The south wall of the chancel has Norman herringbone masonry and there is a small early window on the north side. There are renewed 14th century windows in the nave, one of which has stained glass of c1360 with the quartered arms of the Fitzalans and de Warennes, a three-light 15th century east window, and a three-light west window for which money was left in 1534. The bell-cote is 19th century.

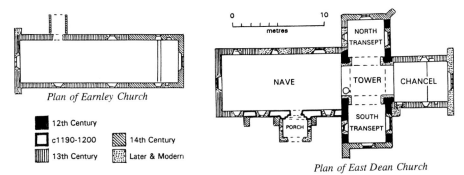

Plan of Earnley Church

■ 12th Century

□ c1190-1200   ▨ 14th Century

▥ 13th Century   ▦ Later & Modern

Plan of East Dean Church

EAST GRINSTEAD   *St Swithun*   TQ 396380

The old church was mostly destroyed when its tower collapsed in 1785 and was replaced by a building designed by James Wyatt with arcades of five bays and battlements on the aisles and above the round clerestory windows. The tower bears the dates 1789 over the west doorway and 1813 higher up. There are brasses of two hen in armour, successive husbands of Dame Elizabeth Grey, d1505, and a civilian of c1520. There are also tablets to Lord Abergavenny, d1744, and Gibbs Crawfurd, d1793, plus cast-iron slabs of 1570 and 1616 with lettering across them.

EAST LAVANT   *St Mary*   SU 862085

The Norman nave has clasping west buttresses and a west doorway with chevrons on the outer arch and one order of columns. Of the four arches of the north arcade the middle two are 13th century. The aisle and chancel are of the restoration of 1863 by G.M.Mills. The south transeptal tower of brick with round arched windows and clasping corner buttresses is of 1671. Reset in the tower east wall is a 14th century tomb recess from the chancel. In the chancel are five stalls with plain misericords.

East Lavant Church

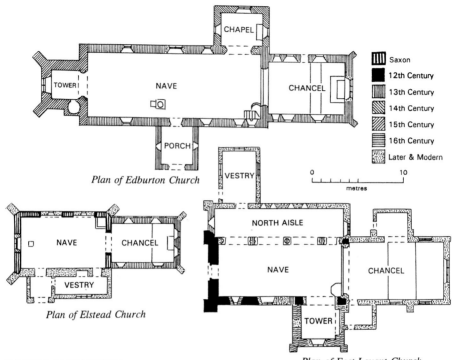

Plan of Edburton Church

Plan of Elstead Church

Plan of East Lavant Church

EAST LAVINGTON   *St Peter*   SU 946163

This 13th century church was mostly rebuilt by G.E.Street in the mid 19th century. Original are the arches into the south transept and chancel and the north aisle with two tiny lancets in the thin outer wall and an arcade of two wide arches of double-chamfered arches with an octagonal pier. The narrower arch further west suggests a NW tower was intended but the wall thicknesses make it unlikely one was built.

EAST MARDEN   *St Peter*   SU 807146

The west part of the single chamber is Norman. The east end may replace an apse and is a 13th century chancel with two lancets on each side and three in the east wall. The goblet-shaped font is probably late 12th century.

EAST PRESTON   *St Mary*   TQ 065026

The nave has remains of a Norman north doorway. The 13th century chancel has three widely spaced east lancets with moulded rere-arches and shafts with stiff-leaf capitals. The tall 15th century west tower has a tower arch with continuous mouldings. It had a spire until 1951. The south aisle is a 19th century addition.

EAST WITTERING   *The Assumption*   SU 802979

The fine Norman south doorway has an outer order of chevrons set on columns with scalloped capitals. The chancel arch is 13th century. The other features are of the restoration of 1875.

EDBURTON   *St Andrew*   TQ 233115

The long nave with large lancets and a contemporary lead font with arcading and low relief scrolls, and the chancel, also with lancets and a trefoil-headed piscina, are all mid 13th century. A north chapel with windows with trefoiled lights was added to serve a chantry founded in 1320 and the spacious porch with a superb view of the Downs may also be of that period. The diagonally buttressed west tower is 15th century. The pulpit, altar rail, and bible in a case are probably of the time of Charles I. In the nave is a memorial to William Hippesley, d1657.

EGDEAN   *St Bartholomew*   SU 995201

Restoration has removed the features of the church built in 1622 except for a brick four-centred south doorway, the chancel arch, also of brick, and the octagonal font and the altar rail.

ELSTEAD   *St Paul*   SU 816198

The west, north, and east walls of the nave have late 11th century herringbone masonry. The chancel arch and the two blocked round arches of a former north aisle are 12th century. The 13th century chancel has two lancet to the north and east and one lancet and a two-light window to the south. This part remained roofed after the church was abandoned in the 1850s and the nave roof and south wall were destroyed by a falling tree in 1893. The new church at Treyford was itself demolished in 1951 and that at Elstead was restored and the nave south side given a porch with a vestry in the form of a lean-to aisle east of it, whilst a hexagonal window was inserted in the west wall.

East Preston Church

FELPHAM   *St Mary*   SZ 948998

Norman work remains in the nave and there are a north arcade and arcaded square font bowl of c1200. Of the 13th century are the south arcade with double-chamfered arches, and the clerestory. The chancel was built c1350 by Shaftsbury Abbey and has tall two-light windows on the north and south sides and a three-light east window with curvilinear tracery. In the 15th century the south aisle was heightened with new windows and flint and brown sandstone chequerwork, and the west tower added. There is a 13th century chest.

FERNHURST   *St Margaret*   SU 899285

Norman masonry remains in the chancel, where there is one original window, and in the nave north wall, with one pilaster buttress. The building of a south aisle in 1859 by Henry Woodyer, and the adding of a tower beyond the aisle and a general restoration of 1881 by Anthony Salvin have removed anything else of interest.

FERRING   *St Andrew*   TQ 094025

The roughcast probably hides Norman walling. Of the mid 13th century are the south aisle with a four bay arcade of double-chamfered arches on circular piers and the chancel east end with an arrangement of lancets with shafted and arcaded rere-arches cut into by a three-light 15th century window. The aisle has an internal buttress in which is a trefoil-headed stoup., whilst the chancel has a restored square piscina with nailhead ornamentation. There are monuments to Thomas Oliver, d1782, and Thomas Richardson, d1797.

FINDON   *St John the Baptist*   TQ 116085

It was probably in the 15th century that a huge new roof with tie-beams and king-posts was built across the Norman nave and a wide 13th century north aisle which has replaced a narrower aisle of c1180-90 with plain pointed arcade arches. A similar arch leads into the south transept although the transept walls are probably older than the 1180s. In the transept east wall is a horseshoe-shaped arch with a billet ornament on the hood-mould. This arch probably led to an apse (unless it is the original chancel arch reset) and was converted into a recess in which is a round stone with floral patterns, possibly originally a boss from a vault. The north chancel and the west tower with lancets and a broach-spire are 13th century. Also of that period are the chancel arch and the much restored screen with rings on the shafts. There is a battered old font in the aisle but that now in use is probably of the time of Sir George Gilbert Scott's restoration of 1867.

FISHBOURNE   *St Peter and St Mary*   SU 842044

The church has a nave with a tiny bell-turret perched on its roof and two separately gabled aisles. The north porch is of 1821 and the south aisle and much of the rest is of the restoration of 1847, but the chancel contains a 13th century lancet.

FITTLEWORTH   *St Mary*   TQ 011192

In 1871 Henry Woodyer replaced a timber framed nave by an aisled structure but the chancel with three east lancets and the west tower with a broach-spire are 13th century. The octagonal 14th century font has rosettes on it. There are painted Royal Arms of George III.

Porch at Ford

Findon Church

FORD   *St Andrew*   TQ 003037

This church has become redundant and was undergoing conservation in 1999. The nave and chancel (plus a square font bowl) are probably late 11th century, with two tiny windows of that date, plus to larger and later Norman windows. There is a star-shaped ornament on the imposts of the plain chancel arch. The three-light east window with reticulated tracery is mid 14th century, whilst the west window is probably a generation or two later. The brick south porch with a Dutch gable is of 1637. Above the vestry doorway is a section of Saxon interlace. The faded 15th century wall-paintings include a Last Judgement over the chancel arch and the Agony on the Garden in a window embrasure on the south side.

FUNTINGTON   *St Mary*   SU 801082

The four-bay north arcade is 13th century, some old work may survive in the north and south chapels, and the diagonally buttressed west tower is 15th century. The south arcade and all the windows are of the drastic restoration of 1859. Parts of the panelling of a 15th century tomb chest are built into the south porch.

Goring Church

Fittleworth Church

Hardham Church

Tower at Henfield

GORING-BY-SEA   *St Mary*   TQ 111026

Much of the church dates from a rebuilding of 1837 by Decimus Bartin. Old features are the late 12th century arcades with pointed single-chamfered arches on piers with scalloped capitals, brasses of a man and wife of the Coke family, c1490, a tablet probably of c1740 to Susan Cook, d1707, and perhaps the tiny bell-turret.

GRAFFHAM   *St Giles*   SU 929167

Old parts which survived the rebuilding of 1874-87 by G.E.Street are the late 12th century arcades with single-chamfered arches on circular piers with scalloped capitals, the fine 13th century west doorway, and a 13th century piscina in the vestry, the old door of which has a lock with a key with heads of a king and queen.

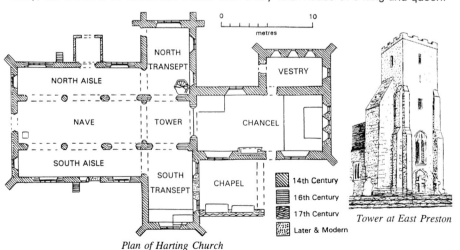

Tower at East Preston

Plan of Harting Church

GREATHAM   *Dedication Unknown*   TQ 044160

This is a delightful, unrestored single chamber with a slate-hung bell-turret. There are two lancets at the east end, and others in the side walls but they are probably later insertions into 12th century walling. Inside are a rustic 17th century altar rail with a crenellated top, and a two decker pulpit of c1820.

HARDHAM   *St Botolph*   TQ 039175

The 11th century nave and chancel have recently been re-whitewashed outside except for the dressed stones of the openings. Two tiny original windows remain. The chancel has a late 13th century east window and a 14th century south window, below which on the outside can be seen remains of a squint looking towards the altar from an anchorite's cell, known to have been occupied by Prior Richard of Lewes in the days before his death in 1285. The octagonal font and the plain bench ends are 15th century. The altar rail is dated 1720 but looks a century older.

During a restoration of 1866, when the bell-turret perched in the nave east gable and the north porch were added, a fine set of early 12th century wall-paintings were exposed. Most of them are now very faded. The nave has the Torments of the Dammed on the west wall, Nativity scenes above the earliest representation in Britain of St George on the north wall, more Nativity scenes above an unidentifiable scene on the south wall, whilst on the east wall are Christ with the Doctors, censing angels, the Annunciation and Visitation, and what is probably the Baptism of Christ. The chancel has Elders and Apostles above the Betrayal and Last Supper on the north wall, Christ in Glory and the Entombment on the east wall, more Elders and Apostles on the south, and on the west side Eve milking a cow on the north side of the chancel arch and the Temptation of Eve on the south side.

HARTING   *St Mary and St Gabriel*   SU 784194

This cruciform building at South Harting is mostly of the early 14th century, a rarity in Sussex. The chancel has an original NE vestry with diagonal buttresses and is wider than the nave, which presumably stands on 11th century foundations. The south transept has diagonal buttresses and a south window with intersecting tracery. The north transept has angle buttresses and a window with tracery with trefoils and a spherical triangle. The nave has aisles with arcades of three bays. The lower arches of the east bay are of after a fire in 1576. Also of that period are the arches under the tower, the aisle windows and mid-wall buttresses, the tomb chest in the chancel south wall, and all the roofs, with king-posts in the nave, trussed rafters in the transepts, and tie-beams and collar beams in the chancel. Three effigies of c1600 and a fourth of Sir Richard Caryll, d1616, have been brought into the south transept from the now-ruined Caryll chapel of 1610 east of the transept. The effigies lay in the recesses surviving in the chapel south wall. Also in the south transept is a late 13th century figure of the Virgin, possibly of Spanish origin. The font has an arcaded 13th century bowl and a Jacobean cover with a central spike and four scrolly brackets.

HENFIELD   *St Peter*   TQ 213163

The four-bay arcades and the chancel arch are 13th century. More impressive are the 15th century west tower and north chapel, the latter with a five-light east window and a four-light north window. The other features are mostly of the restoration of 1870 by Slater and Carpenter.

HEYSHOTT   *St James*   SU 897181

The nave with an original doorway, and the three bay north arcade of double-chamfered arches on circular piers are 13th century. Of the 14th century are the nave west and south windows. The chancel and north aisle were rebuilt larger than before in the 19th century and a vestry then added. The chancel south window probably reproduces a 15th century window here. The mutilated 13th century font has a 17th century cover. There are 18th century painted Royal Arms over the south doorway.

HORSHAM   *St Mary*   TQ 171303

The lower stage of the tower with heavy clasping buttresses (one contains a staircase) is Norman. It lies off-centre to the wide nave, yet the presence of a Norman window and doorway in the north aisle makes it unlikely that the north arcade lies beyond the position of the Norman nave north wall. There is now no break between the early 13th century five bay aisled nave and the late 13th century three bay aisled chancel with a huge 15th century east window renewed in 1865. Additions to the already spacious 13th century church are a porch and north chapel beyond the north aisle built to contain a chantry founded in 1307 and having a three bay arcade, a 15 century NE vestry, a chapel for a chantry of 1447 beside the south aisle of the chancel, and the five bay outer south aisle added by Teulon in 1865 with a vestry west of it, looking into which the south aisle has one 13th century lancet.

The stained glass is all 19th century but the many monuments include an effigy of the priest Thomas Clark, a brass of a 15th century lady, a stone effigy of Thomas de Braose, d1395, an altar tomb of Thomas Hoo, d1485, an effigy of Elizabeth Delves, d1654, plus many 18th century tablets now gathered under the tower.

Horsham Church

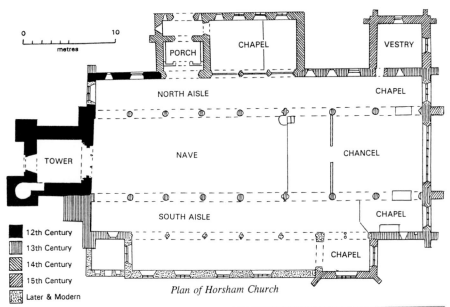

Plan of Horsham Church

0 —— 10
metres

- 12th Century
- 13th Century
- 14th Century
- 15th Century
- Later & Modern

PORCH CHAPEL VESTRY

NORTH AISLE CHAPEL

TOWER NAVE CHANCEL

SOUTH AISLE CHAPEL

CHAPEL

HOUGHTON   *St Nicholas*

TQ 020116

The church was mostly rebuilt in 1857 but the south doorway with a stop-chamfer is original 13th century work and the three east lancets must reproduce originals. The font is probably 17th century.

HURSTPIERPOINT   *Holy Trinity*

TQ 271165

The only relics of what existed before the rebuilding of 1843-5 by Sir Charles Barry are an effigy of a 13th century cross-legged knight in the south chapel, an effigy with contemporary railings of a late 14th century knight in the north aisle NW corner, a number of 13th and 14th century tiles lying outside the west doorway, and the 15th to 17th century stained glass medallions collected by Bishop Rother of Durham in the mid 18th century set in two of the windows.

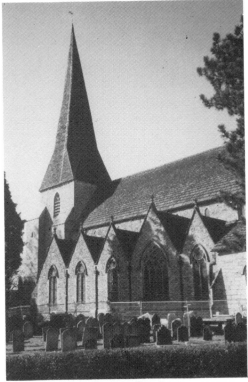

Horsham Church

Interior of Isfield Church

IFIELD   *St Margaret*   TQ 247376

The short chancel has 13th century lancets, and others remain in the aisle west walls, so the nave may always have been as wide as it is now. The arcades and the chancel arch are all 14th century, but the north arcade probably a generation earlier than its southern counterpart. Many of the windows, including the clerestory, are 14th century, whilst others are 15th century. The west tower is of 1883. The square font with four corner shafts with waterleaf capitals is late 12th century. The lectern has been made up of 17th century carved fragments including caryatids. There are effigies thought to be of Sir John de Ifelde, c1340, and Lady Margaret Ifelde, d1347.

ITCHINGFIELD   *St Nicholas*   TQ 131289

Until Scott added the south aisle in 1865, this was a single chamber with a timber framed 15th century west tower, shingled above the lean-to abutments to the north and south. The nave has one tiny Norman window. Larger and later Norman windows have been reset in the north wall of the chancel of 1713. Under one of them on the south is a 14th century "low-side" window. Another 14th century window in the nave west wall now looks into the tower. In the churchyard is a timber framed building, partly 15th century and partly c1600, thought to have originally been used as accommodation for a visiting priest sent over from Sele Priory to take services.

KEYMER   *St Cosmas and St Damian*   TQ 315153

The church was entirely rebuilt in 1866 by E.E.Scott except for the Norman apse.

Timber tower at Itchingfield

Apse at Keymer

KINGSTON BUCI   *St Julian*   TQ 236052

The nave is probably early 11th century Saxon work. Apart from a few late medieval windows the rest is 13th century and consists of a narrow north aisle with a two bay arcade and lighted only by a single west lancet, a central tower with a rib-vault and three orders of chamfered arches to east and west, and a chancel with lancets. The delightful interior is dominated by an 18th century two-decker pulpit incorporating 16th century linenfold panels. There are two medieval bench ends, box pews and a rare Jacobean singing desk. The 14th century screen has been much restored. On the north side of the chancel is a Lewknor family tomb serving as an Easter Sepulchre and having defaced scenes of the Resurrection, Pieta and Holy Trinity.

KIRDFORD   *St John the Baptist*   TQ 018265

The nave has a blocked Norman south doorway of two orders with cushion-capitals on the columns. The north aisle with a three bay arcade is 13th century, but the aisle east window is 14th century. Of the 15th century are the west tower with angle buttresses and a tower arch of three orders, several windows in the chancel and aisle, and the vestry north of the chancel, with a tunnel vault with thick chamfered ribs. The bell-openings of the tower have lost their tracery. The porch in front of the tower is partly late medieval and partly Elizabethan. A 19th century restoration renewed the 13th century chancel arch and provided new south windows. The octagonal font is of 1620. The benches in the north aisle are probably 16th century. The altar rail is late 17th century. One north lancet contains original locally made coloured glass.

Porch at Lancing

Lancing Church

LANCING   *St James The Less*   TQ 182056

The aisles have three bay arcades with double-chamfered arches on octagonal piers to the nave and then extend further east to flank a plain pyramidal-roofed central tower (lowered in 1618), beyond which is a two bay chancel with trefoiled lancets in blind arcading and an ogival headed recess beyond. Much of the building is early 14th century, but the two end walls are Norman, and the outer arch of the south porch has a fine portal of c1200 with roll-mouldings and columns with stiff foliage on the capitals. The square-headed aisle windows are mostly renewed. The nave has a fine king-post roof. The Norman font is square with square panels on the sides. In the 15th century the northern arch of the crossing was blocked and the aisle there shortened to make space for a stair-turret.

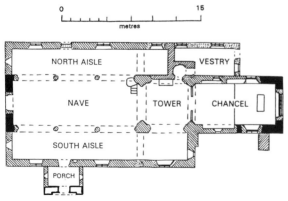

Plan of Lancing Church

*Saxon stone
at Jevington*

LINCH   *St Luke*   TQ 862275

The south doorway is the principal relic of a small church of 1705 enlarged and altered in 1886 by Lacy W.Ridge. There are two small stained glass panels of the Descent from the Cross and the Ascension, probably 15th century German work.

LINCHMERE   *St Peter*   TQ 870319

The Norman nave has a rounded-headed west doorway and a reset window towards the inner aisle added in 1856 by Woodyer. In 1906 P.M.Johnston added an outer aisle with a wooden arcade. The 13th century chancel has several lancets and an east window of two lancets under a circle. Tall columns support a slender bell-turret at the west end. This is probably of 1654, the year given on the attached sundial. There is an Italian relief of c1300 showing the Seven Deadly Sins.

LINDFIELD   *St John Baptist*   TQ 349259

The church is mostly of the early 14th century and has a font with cusped ogee panels of that period. There are transepts, aisles which engage the angle-buttressed west tower and consequently have arcades of two and a half bays, a large two storey porch on the south side, and a chancel with a restored east window. The chancel chapels with two bay arcades of four-centred arches with piers of the four-shafts and four hollows type are of c1500, and there are windows of that period in the diagonally buttressed south transept. The irregularly shaped south chapel has two corbels in the form of angels in the south wall.

Interior of Lindfield Church

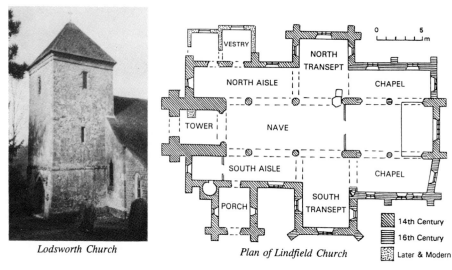

Lodsworth Church

Plan of Lindfield Church

14th Century
16th Century
Later & Modern

LODSWORTH   *St Peter*   SW 931228

The church was given a neo-Norman south transept in 1840 and then was later given aisles. The NW corner is the main survival of a late 11th century nave, and there is a west tower of c1300 with a worn west doorway with nook-shafts.

LOXWOOD   *St John Baptist*   TQ 041310

In the north aisle of the brick church of 1898 by Roland Plumbe with a north tower are several medieval benches with knobs on ends of unequal projection.

LURGASHALL   *St Laurence*   SU 938273

The 11th century nave has a pilaster buttress on each side and original windows on the north. On the south side is a timber-framed gallery which eventually became the village school and there is a south transeptal tower probably of the late 14th century with a spire. The 13th century chancel with two lancets on the south side was repaired in 1731. The east wall is mid 19th century but must reproduce the original layout. The unusual square rusticated font bowl is dated 1661. There is a Baroque style tablet to William Yaldwyn, d1728.

LYMINSTER   *St Mary Magdalene*   TQ 022048

The nave and chancel are both Saxon and were used by a Benedictine nunnery. The arch between the two parts is typically tall and narrow. One spandrel of the late 12th century north arcade contains the head of a Saxon window and the head of a doorway appears above a blocked Norman doorway on the south side, next to which is an unusual sexfoiled window of the late 13th century. Windows like this one appear occasionally in clerestories but never normally in a tall blank wall such as this. The arcade pier capitals have scallops and an early form of stiff-leaf and the aisle has a trefoil-headed piscina. The aisle roof is late medieval. An early 12th century doorway faces west into a 13th century tower. The chancel also has 13th century lancets. The east window and tower top stage are 15th century.

MADEHURST   *St Mary Magdalene*   SU 984099

A rebuilding of 1864 by T.G.Jackson has left only a plain Norman west doorway and a 14th century window in the nave as the only ancient features.

MERSTON   *St Giles*   SU 894026

The 13th century nave and chancel form one chamber and its roof sweeps down over the aisle almost to the ground so that there are no north windows. There is a trefoil headed piscina. The four bay arcade is also probably 13th century. The west window is 15th century and the east window is 19th century. The brick porch has a tie-beam dated 1637. The Norman font has shallow arcading on each side.

MIDHURST   *St Mary Magdalene and St Denys*   SU 887215

The south transeptal tower has a 13th century base. It is longer from north to south than it is east-west. The top dates from the 16th century when the nave and chancel were provided with new arcades of double-chamfered arches on octagonal piers. The north aisle and the chapels were additions of that period. Most of the exterior was renewed by Lacy W.Ridge in 1882 and the Cowdray monuments were taken off to Easebourne. There are painted Royal Arms of Queen Anne.

Round window at Lyminster

Midhurst Church

MID LAVANT   *St Nicholas*   SU 855086

The nave has one Norman south window, and the chancel has several 13th century lancets and a piscina. The three arches of equal width between the two parts, the north aisle, south porch and the bell-turret with a broach-spire are 19th century, when a monument to Dame Mary May, d1681, was hidden under a new floor.

MILLAND   *St Luke*   SU 824282

Behind the new church of 1878 with a large west tower is the single chamber old chapel, probably 16th century but possibly later. The south doorway and porch and the east and west windows are original. The north transept is early 19th century. The interior has box pews and a plain 18th century pulpit.

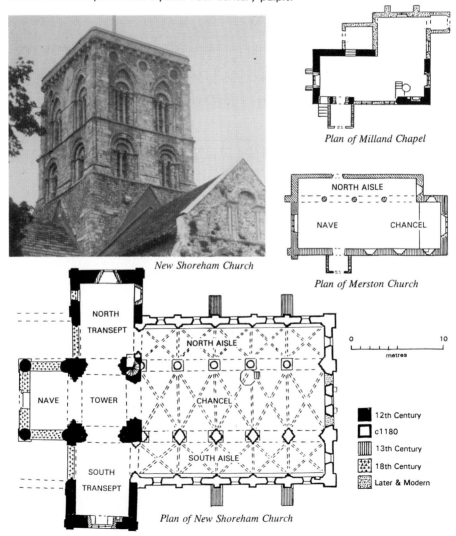

Plan of Milland Chapel

NORTH AISLE

NAVE   CHANCEL

Plan of Merston Church

New Shoreham Church

NORTH
TRANSEPT

NORTH AISLE

NAVE   TOWER   CHANCEL

SOUTH AISLE

SOUTH
TRANSEPT

0   10
metres

■ 12th Century
□ c1180
▦ 13th Century
▨ 18th Century
▩ Later & Modern

Plan of New Shoreham Church

interior of New Shoreham Church

NEW SHOREHAM   *St Mary de Haura*   TQ 216052

This impressive church recalls that at Boxgrove. It has a crossing and transepts of the 1130s, a grand, fully-aisled chancel and upper stage of the tower of the 1170s and 80s, and a nave which has been truncated and ruined since it was damaged either during a French raid of 1628 or the Civil War of the 1640s. Just one bay of the six of this Norman nave now remains in use, having been patched up in the 18th century without its aisles and a doorway moved into it from elsewhere. The transepts have upper windows with shafts and on the south is a triplet of arches. The east walls have scars of chapels. The central apse which existed before the new chancel was built was traced in 1915. The lowest stage of the tower above the crossing has two-light windows of the 1130s. The upper stage has tall three-light bell-openings with pointed outer arches, giving a particularly fine effect.

The chancel is five bays long and has a quadripartite vault carried on shafts rising from the piers on the south but corbelled out above them on the north, clear evidence of a change of plan during construction. Probably it was only originally intended to vault the aisles. To help carry the weight of the high vault there are flying arches down onto two massive buttresses added at a slightly later date on each side. The arcades have richly moulded pointed arches with one keeled order and are set on alternately round and octagonal piers with stiff-leaf capitals on the north side, whilst the slightly later south side has compound piers. There is then a triforium stage with pairs of pointed arches and then a clerestory of large single lancets. The details are mostly Transitional but purely Norman motifs occur in the blank arcading of the aisle walls which were the first parts to be built. The aisles now have 19th century neo-Norman windows replacing larger, later medieval windows.

The Norman font bowl with ornamental patterns on each side sits on a stem and corner shafts which are too big for it. The monuments include mid 15th century brasses of a man and wife, and several tablets of c1800 in the north transept.

NEWTIMBER   *St John Baptist*   TQ 271135

The nave and chancel have 13th century walling but the restoration of 1875 by Carpenter and Ingelow has removed everything of interest except a Jacobean pulpit and an 18th century tablet to the Osborne family. The Gothick tower is of 1839.

NORTH CHAPEL   *St John the Baptist*   SU 935294

The square font with pilaster strips is dated 1662. The west tower is early 19th century. The rest was entirely rebuilt by Anthony Salvin in 1877.

NORTH MARDEN   *St Mary*   SU 808161

This is a small single chamber of the 1130s with a south doorway with one order of chevrons enclosing balls and an apsidal east end. Just three other English parish churches preserve this Norman plan form intact. Only the west window is original but the 19th century openings are of Norman form. There is a trefoiled 13th century piscina in the apse, and there are a small set of Royal Arms of George III in iron.

NORTH MUNDHAM   *St Stephen*   SU 874021

The restoration of 1883 by A.W.Blomfield saw the chancel rebuilt and given flanking chambers to contain a vestry and organ, whilst most of the windows were renewed. There is a diagonally-buttressed 16th century west tower in which a 13th century doorway has been reset. The aisles are 13th century with original west lancets. Both arcades have double-chamfered arches but on the south one chamfer is hollowed, so this side is a generation later. A panel from a monument of c1500 reset in the south porch is thought to have had kneeling figures on either side of a central symbol.

North Mundham Church

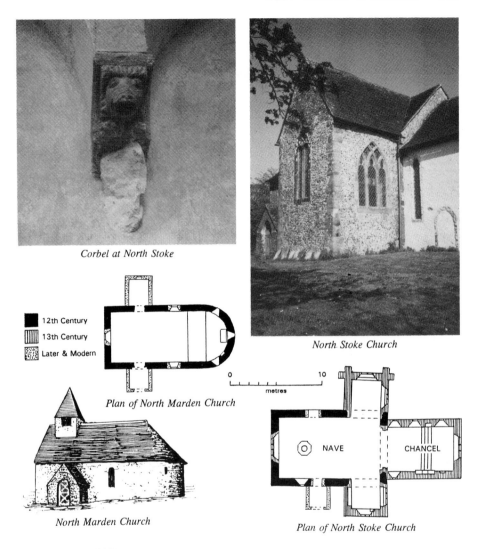

Corbel at North Stoke

12th Century
13th Century
Later & Modern

North Stoke Church

Plan of North Marden Church

0   10
metres

North Marden Church

Plan of North Stoke Church

NORTH STOKE   *Dedication Unknown*   TQ 020108

This is a delightfully unrestored church with a Norman nave with one original window on each side. The 13th century chancel has sedilia and a piscina and two lancets on the south and three lancets and an aumbry on the north. The three east lancets are 19th century, but are flanked by original image brackets with stiff-leaf. The transepts were added in the 1290s and have windows with Geometrical style tracery. A small timber bell-turret is perched on top of the north transept, which is more square than its counterpart, with angle buttresses, possibly with an intention of making it a tower. The chancel arch is 14th century and has above it floral wall-paintings. There is a bulbous font of c1200. There is are early 14th century scenes of the Coronation of the Virgin in the east windows of both the chancel and the south transept.

NUTHURST   *St Andrew*   TQ 192262

The wide nave and chancel are both 14th century but much restored. The nave has paired cusped lancets, the chancel an east window with reticulated tracery containing fragments of original glass showing Christ in Majesty and censing angels, whilst between them is a double-chamfered chancel arch. The north vestry is of 1907.

OLD SHOREHAM   *St Nicholas*   TQ 208060

There is Saxon work, supposedly 9th century, at the west end, with a blocked doorway facing north. This west end is narrower than the rest of the Norman nave and suggests a possible former west tower. A blocked Norman doorway survives in the north wall. In the 1150s a central tower and transepts were added, the crossing arches having roll-mouldings and chevrons on stepped piers with half-round shafts with scallops and heads on the capitals. There are outer labels with billets, shells and rosettes. The transepts have clasping pilaster corner buttresses and had chapels opening off to the east. The Norman-looking windows piercing central pilasters are of the restoration of 1839-40 by J.M.Neale and J.C.Buckler, when all the windows were replaced except those of two lights in the bell-stage of the tower. These are flanked by blank arches and there are round openings above. The chancel was enlarged c1300 and gained a tomb recess in the south wall and a tie-beam with dog-tooth. The north chapel was also rebuilt. Only its piscina and the 12th and 14th century arches to it from the transept and chancel now remain. A smaller 19th century structure now stands here, with a vestry beyond it. The much restored screen is early 14th century. There is a rustic tablet to William Monk, d1714, and also a monument to Colvill Bridger, d1797 and his descendants.

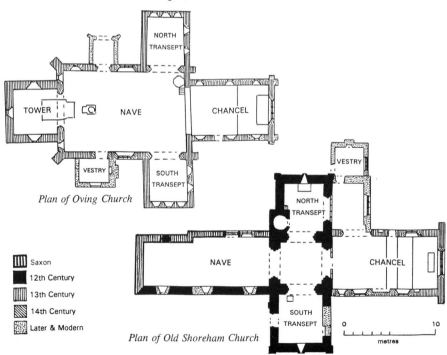

Plan of Oving Church

|||| Saxon

■ 12th Century

||||| 13th Century

▨ 14th Century

▦ Later & Modern

Plan of Old Shoreham Church

0   10
metres

Crossing arches, Old Shoreham

Oving Church

OVING   *St Andrew*   SU 901055

This is essentially an all-13th century church of nave, chancel, transepts and west tower with a broach-spire. The nave is so wide that it is possible that arcades have been removed. This would explain why the arches to the transepts are 14th century insertions. The south doorway now opening into a Victorian vestry and a window beside it are also 14th century, but original is the fine north doorway with two orders of columns and complex mouldings on the arch. There are many lancets, some renewed, with stepped groups of three in the transept end walls. Norman fragments carved with chevrons are set into the north transept west wall.

Interior of Pagham Church

PAGHAM   *St Thomas Becket*   SZ 884975

The chancel has 11th century herringbone masonry on the south side but is mostly early 13th century with three lancets on each side and three more facing east. Some 13th century walling remains in the south transept but the north transept, the aisles and the nave west wall were rebuilt in 1837 by John Elliot. West of the renewed transept arches are plain sections of walling and then arcades of three bays of c1230 on the south and two bays of c1200-10 on the north. On that side a third bay with scalloped capitals opens into a NW tower of c1200 with pilaster buttresses. At the east end is 16th century Flemish glass from a church in Rouen showing the Adoration of the Child, the Adoration of the Magi and the Presentation in the Temple.

PARHAM   *St Peter*   TQ 059141

The church lies on a lawn beside the house. The tower base is 15th century, the circular lead font has strips of inscription with the arms of Andrew Peverel, Knight of the Shire in 1351, and the south chapel is of 1545. There is a blocked two bay arcade on the north side. The tower top and the interior were part of a drastic remodelling c1820 from which date the box pews, pulpit, fretwork screen, the coved ceiling of the nave and the panelled plaster vaults of the chancel and the north transept containing the squire's pew with the luxury of a fireplace.

PATCHING   *St John*   TQ 087065

The nave and chancel and north transeptal tower are all 13th century with many lancets and an original nave roof with tie-beams and king-posts. The chancel has a trefoiled piscina with stiff-leaf capitals and is out of line with the nave. The tower has arches of two orders to the east and west as well as one with a roll-moulding to the south so it must have originally been a central tower. The bell-stage has coupled lancets. The octagonal 15th century font has quatrefoil panels with rosettes. The 19th century pulpit incorporates early 16th century arabesque panels.

PETWORTH   *St Mary*   SU 976219

The lower part of the south transeptal tower with a SE stair turret is 15th century. The brick top stage was added in 1827 by Sir Charles Barry. His spire was removed in 1947 and the present parapet and roof are of 1953. The chancel has south windows of c1260 with two lights under a big roundel. The arches of the north arcade and the octagonal font with quatrefoils are 14th century. The other features are of the 1820s and another restoration of 1903 by Kempe and Tower. In an aumbry is an early 16th century panel of the Virgin and Child from Flanders or France. The monuments include kneeling effigies of Sir John Dawtry, d1542, and his wife, a cartouche to John Peachey, d1693, a memorial with a cherub to John Wickins, d1783, and his wife Philadelphia, and several 18th century tablets in the chancel.

POLING   *St Nicholas*   TQ 047047

The Saxon nave retains one double-splayed window high up on the north side. Preserved below it is its original wooden shutter. The two bay south arcade is of c1300 and the chancel is of the 1380s, whilst the angle-buttressed west tower and several windows in the aisles are 15th century. The east window is of 1830. There is a medieval screen with above it a rood beam thought to be from Bargham church. The font may be Saxon. There is a brass to the mid 15th century vicar Walter Davy.

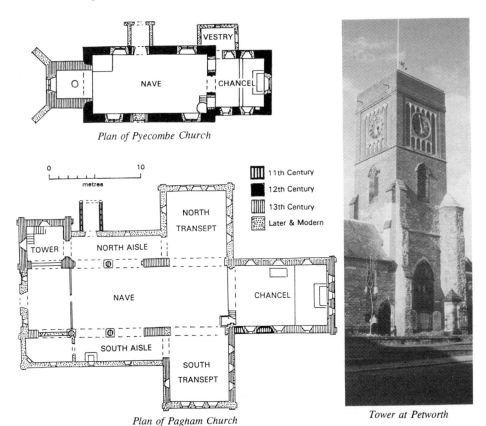

Plan of Pyecombe Church

‖‖‖	11th Century
■	12th Century
‖‖‖	13th Century
▨	Later & Modern

Plan of Pagham Church

Tower at Petworth

Pulborough Church

Poynings Church

POYNINGS   *Holy Trinity*   TQ 265121

Michael Poynings, d1369, left money for the complete rebuilding of the church, which is entirely of that period except for the south transept end window of the 1640s brought here from Chichester Cathedral. The church is cruciform with a central tower with very modest openings, a chancel and north transept which are diagonally buttressed and a nave and south transept which are angle-buttressed, plus a porch on the north side. The windows, mostly of two lights, but of five in the east wall, have early Perpendicular style tracery. Original features are the ogival-arched sedilia and piscina in the chancel, the octagonal font with ogival-headed arcading, and the screen, whist several windows contain 15th century stained glass. Of the 17th century are the Jacobean pulpit, the altar rail and two family pews.

East window at Poynings

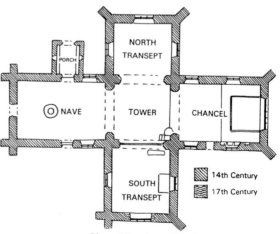

Plan of Poynings Church

Sedilia at Poynings

Pyecombe Church

PULBOROUGH   *St Mary*   TQ 046187

Money was left for building the angle-buttressed and embattled west tower in 1404. It was intended to be vaulted. Another bequest dates the nave with a clerestory and aisles to the 1420s. The aisle windows are of two lights subdividing into four under the segmental head with a label. The tower arch has three continuous chamfers and there are four bay arcades with double-chamfered arches on piers with four shafts and four hollows. There are north and south porches and a fine king-post roof. One 14th century window is re-used in the south aisle east wall. The late 13th century chancel has three east lancets under one rere-arch with mouldings and shafts and a piscina, but the ogee-headed sedilia are later. The north chapel is also 13th century and has a two bay arcade to the chancel. There is a Norman font with arcading. There are brasses of the 1450s and 1480s in the south aisle and a finer brass to Thomas Harlyng, d1423, in the north aisle. In the north chapel is a 15th century tomb chest. There is also a tablet to the Reverend Harvey Spragg, d1796.

PYECOMBE   *The Transfiguration*   TQ 292126

The nave and chancel are both Norman with a plain round arch between them, and also of that period is the drum-shaped lead font with double scrolls in arcading, trefoil-headed arcading, and a band of fluting. The pyramidal-roofed west tower is 13th century. Most of the windows are 19th century. The pulpit is of 1636 and there is similar woodwork incorporated in the reader's desk.

Interior of Pulborough Church

Racton Church

RACTON   *Dedication Unknown*   SU 779093

The church has a 12th century nave and 13th century chancel of equal length divided by a tympanum over a tie-beam. There are Royal Arms of the 18th century. The windows, including one of the 15th century in the east wall, have been renewed. On the north side is a canopied tomb chest of c1520, probably that of Hugh Gounter. There is a bas-relief of the deceased and his family. There are also kneeling figures under a canopy of Sir George Gounter, d1624, and his wife, and a bust in a frame to Sir Charles Nicholl, d1733.

ROGATE   *St Bartholomew*   SU 808238

The chancel and the aisled nave are mostly 13th century but the external walls have been mostly rebuilt whilst the presence of one round arch on the north side suggests remnants of earlier work. There are damaged sedilia in the chancel. The rebuilt 14th century north chapel has an arch to the chancel with continuous mouldings. There also was once a 14th century east window. At the west end an aisle-less bay contains massive corner posts and diagonal braces to support the bell-turret.

RUDGEWICK   *Holy Trinity*   TQ 091344

The nave south wall is probably Norman and the tower may be early 13th century. The north aisle and the chancel are early 14th century with tall two-light windows with trefoils and spherical triangles in the tracery, the aisle windows having small heads as label-stops. The arcade arches have a complex section. The chancel has original piscina and aumbry but the east window has been renewed externally. The square Norman font has round-headed arcading and a moulded base.

Rustington Church

RUSPER *St Mary Magdalene* TQ 205374

The large west tower is probably 16th century with 13th century parts re-used and has big buttresses and a square stair-turret. The top and the west window date from 1855 when the rest of the church was rebuilt. There are Royal Arms of George I, and a candelabra given in 1770, plus another thought to be medieval. There are brasses with half-figures of John de Kyggesfold, d1370, and his wife, and full figures of Thomas Challoner, d1532, and his wife.

RUSTINGTON *St Peter and St Paul* TQ 050023

Of the end of the 12th century are the south arcade with plain pointed arches on piers with waterleaves and scalloping, and the west tower with twin round-headed bell-openings under pointed arches with nook-shafts. The north transept and chancel with lancets are 13th century. The east wall has three lancets under a rere-arch with a single lancet above. The north arcade with arches of complex section and probably also the quatrefoil clerestory windows are 14th century. A mid 16th century monument in the transept has kneeling figures and a Crucifixion.

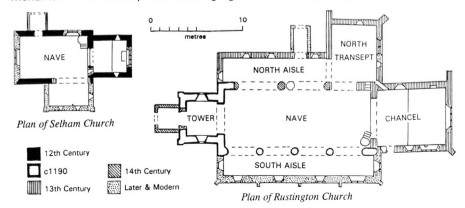

Plan of Selham Church

Plan of Rustington Church

SELHAM   *St James*   SU 932207

This is a small nave-and-chancel chapel probably of the late 11th century since there thin walls have much herringbone masonry. Two tiny windows remain in the chancel. The chancel arch is of exceptional interest and is thought to be a composite of Saxon and Early Norman parts. The arch is roll-moulded and springs from shafts with profusely carved capitals, abaci, and imposts. The interlaced snakes and beast head are in the Viking tradition whilst one abacus has Saxon interlace and the other stylised foliage. The tub font is probably of the same period as the church. There is a later squint beside the chancel arch, and there is a single double-chamfered 13th century arch to a chapel has been rebuilt along with the nave west wall.

SELSEY   *St Peter*   SZ 856937 & 872957

Incorporated in the church of 1865 by J.P.St Aubyn lying in the middle of the village are the arcades from the old church at Church Norton 2km to the NE beside Pagham Harbour. The arcades have three bays of the 1180s with single-chamfered pointed arches and scalloped capitals on the east responds, and a fourth western bay of c1230 with double-chamfered arches. There is also a square font of c1100 with round-arcaded arcading on the stem and four shafts. Until it was dismantled the old church had a diagonally buttressed 16th century west tower and 13th century aisles with west lancets and 15th century north and south windows. The 13th century chancel with lancets, a piscina and a 15th century east window still remains roofed. It contains a tomb with panels showing John Lewis and his wife Agnes, d1537, kneeling towards a missing Trinity or Crucifixion.

SHERMANDBURY   *St Giles*   TQ 115188

The nave was extended in 1710 and again in 1885 but retains traces of a 13th or 14th century north doorway, and there is a font of c1300. The small chancel has the unusual feature of a pair of two-light square-headed windows in the east wall. There are Royal Arms of Queen Anne and box pews with farm names on them.

Selham Church

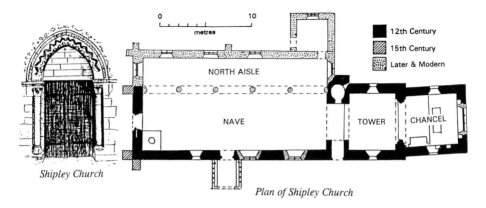

Shipley Church

Plan of Shipley Church

12th Century
15th Century
Later & Modern

NORTH AISLE

NAVE

TOWER

CHANCEL

SHIPLEY *St Mary* TQ 145218

This impressive Norman church is thought to have been built in the 1120s to serve a newly established preceptory of the Knights Templars. It has a long nave, a central tower and a chancel set on a different axis so that it bends to the north. On the south side all three parts have large original windows with double splays, and a doorway with one order of shafts now entered through a 16th century timber porch. Another doorway opens into the south jamb of the very thick arch between the tower and nave. This and the thinner east arch have chevrons on a roll-moulding. The pointed west doorway with more (renewed) chevrons on the arch and columns with waterleaf capitals is of the end of the 12th century. The window above is of c1300. In 1893 the north aisle with a NE vestry beyond it were added by J.L.Pearson and the 16th century east window renewed. The church contains a 13th century reliquary and an alabaster monument with recumbent effigies of Sir Thomas Caryll, d1616, and wife.

Shipley Church

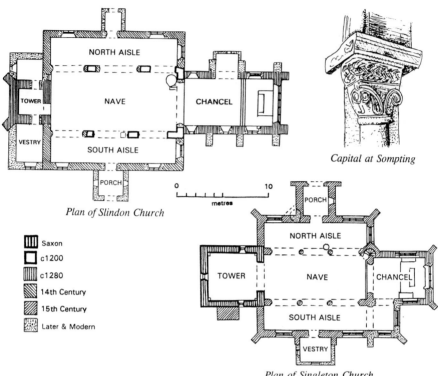

Capital at Sompting

Plan of Slindon Church

Saxon
c1200
c1280
14th Century
15th Century
Later & Modern

Plan of Singleton Church

SIDLESHAM   *St Mary*   SZ 855990

The transepts of c1200 have tall end lancets and blocked arches which led to two-bay eastern aisles. An altar recess has been built where the chancel arch once was for the chancel and a vestry lying to the north of it have been destroyed. The north end of the north transept is railed off for a now-vanished monument. The nave and aisles with three bay arcades are early 13th century. The south aisle retains an original doorway and west and south lancets. Both aisles have 19th century dormer windows. The diagonally buttressed west tower with bricks used for the bell-openings is 16th century. The 13th century font on a stem with four corner shafts is decorated with rosettes.

SINGLETON   *St John Evangelist*   SU 877131

The 11th century west tower has double-splayed windows on three sides and a triangular opening above the tower arch of c1200. The nave walls must be 11th century but are pierced below by three bay 13th century arcades thought to have been remodelled in the 15th century. The chancel arch is also 13th century. The 15th century north porch probably once had an upper storey. There are two-light windows of c1400 in the aisles and three-light 16th century windows in the chancel. A small window over the chancel arch contains old glass. The west gallery is probably 18th century. There are straight-topped 15th century bench ends. In the chancel are two damaged late medieval tomb chests and there is a tablet with interesting inscriptions to the celebrated huntsman Thomas Johnson, d1744.

Singleton Church

SLAUGHAM   *St Mary*   TQ 357281

The Norman nave has a blocked north doorway and there is a font of that period with shallow arcading, a fish and three upright sprays. The late 13th century south aisle has an arcade of two double-chamfered arches and a west lancet but was otherwise rebuilt wider in 1857-60 by Joseph Clarke. His is the upper part of the 13th century west tower. The chancel has a 14th century east window and an arcade of three bays towards a south chapel which was rebuilt in 1613, but given new windows by Clarke. The chapel contains a brass showing John Covert, d1503 under a canopy, and a monument with kneeling figures of Richard Covert, d1579 and his family. In a recess in the chancel are brasses of Richard Covert, d1547 and three wives with a Resurrection scene. Beside it is a monument to Jane Covert, d1586. The 17th century pulpit with columns is a foreign import given to the church in 1890. Also foreign are the early 16th century panels with saints and linenfold.

Interior of Slaugham Church

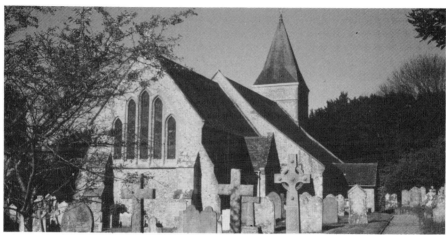

Slindon Church

SLINDON   *St Mary*   SZ 961084

One Early Norman window remains on the north side above the arcade. Pointed arches with two slight chamfers were pierced through the nave walls in the late 12th century for a one bay chapel on the north and a two bay aisle on the south. In the early 14th century another arch was provided on the south and two more on the north to make a regular layout of a fully aisled nave. The 13th century chancel has five stepped lancets in the east wall and others in the side walls, but on the south side one blocked lancet remains of an earlier scheme of c1200. All the windows were renewed outside during a restoration of 1866 by T.G.Jackson, who provided the top of the late 13th century west tower and vestries on either side of it, plus north and south porches. There are slight indications of an abortive late 13th century scheme to build a SW tower. This corner contains old benches with poppy-heads. The square 13th century font has a stem and four corner columns. In the chancel is a wooden effigy of Anthony St Leger, d1539, the only one of its type in Sussex.

Sompting Church

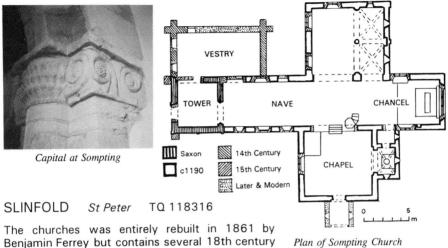

Capital at Sompting

Ⅲ Saxon	▨ 14th Century	
☐ c1190	▨ 15th Century	
	▨ Later & Modern	

Plan of Sompting Church

SLINFOLD   *St Peter*   TQ 118316

The churches was entirely rebuilt in 1861 by Benjamin Ferrey but contains several 18th century tablets under the tower and a worn effigy of a female of c1300, probably one of the Tregoz family.

SOMPTING   *St Mary*   TQ 162056

This church is famous for its tall Saxon west tower of c1000 covered with a gabled pyramidal roof or "Rhemish helm" because of a prevalence of tower like it in the Rhineland. In Britain it is unique, although another one survived in Cambridge until c1800. It has thin pilasters clasping the corners and in the middle of each side and having pairs of triangular-headed bell-openings to the east and west and pairs of two-light round-headed bell-openings to the north and south. The tower arch with leaf capitals id off-centre, possibly to allow room for an altar beside it in the tower. The nave is the same width as the tower and has a blocked north doorway probably of the early 12th century. The rest of the building dates from immediately after the church was granted to the Knights Templars in 1184. They continued the narrow nave eastward into a chancel without division between the two and added a north transept with a rib-vaulted east aisle to accommodate two altars. The arches are pointed but without chamfers and have capitals with scallops. Original windows survive here, but most of the others throughout the church are 15th century. What now serves as a south transept was in fact only connected to the church by an arch in the 19th century. It was a square chapel for the Templars' own use, at a lower level than the rest and having its own south doorway of two orders with a roll-moulding, and a rib vaulted sanctuary projecting on the east with a tiny sacristy tucked between it and the chancel. A doorway was blocked through to the sacristy from the chancel in the 19th century.

After the fall of the Templars in 1306 Sompting was granted to the Knights Hospitallers. They built a large chapel on the north side with a piscina and openings into the nave and tower which remain blocked, since although the chapel was restored from ruin in the 1970s it serves as vestries. In the nave is an early 13th century carved Christ in Majesty with the Signs of the Evangelists around the halo. Near it are two Saxon stones with interlace. There are several Saxon fragments of carving in the chancel, two of them forming a head for the piscina recess. A tomb recess opposite is the monument of Richard Burre, d1527. There is a tablet to John Crofts, d1771, in the north transept along with several other tablets of c1800.

SOUTH BERSTED   *St Mary Magdalene*   SU 935002

The original medieval settlements of North Bersted and South Bersted (which has the church) are now engulfed by Bognor Regis suburbia. The west tower is of c1200, although the heavy west buttresses are later. The five bay arcades of the narrow aisles are of c1240 and have piers alternately round and octagonal and responds with scalloped capitals. The chancel and exterior features of the aisles are of the restoration of 1879-81 by Ewan Christian, the east window with good glass of 1880.

SOUTH STOKE   *St Leonard*   TQ 026100

The nave has Norman south and north doorways, the latter now blocked. One north window may be of c1200. Of the 13th century are the south porch vaulted with chamfered transverse ribs and having tiny triangular buttresses, and what from the inside appears as a nicely composed west front with lancets flanking a thin tower which was given a machicolated top and broach-spire in the 19th century. The east window and several others and the chancel arch are also 19th century.

SOUTHWICK   *St Michael*   TQ 239054

The nave and aisles are of 1834 by John Garrett. The much restored chancel is 13th century with lancets. The west tower with a broach spire was dismantled in 1941 after being damaged by a bomb but was rebuilt in 1949, when vestries were added on either side of it. Originally the tower was 12th and 13th century work although the lower part was thought to be Saxon. The tower arch has volute capitals and there are others on the arcade between the chancel and south chapel.

STEDHAM   *St James*   SU 864226

The church was entirely rebuilt in 1850 by J.Butler except for the plain tower of 1673 and one reset Norman window in the north aisle east wall. Inside is a tablet to the Reverend Thomas Wrench, d1778.

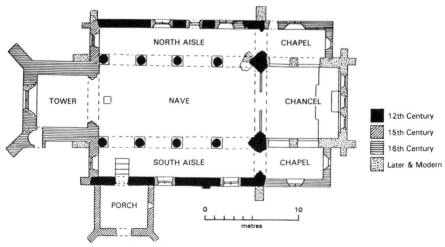

Plan of Steyning Church

Interior of Steyning Church

STEYNING   *St Andrew*   TQ 179114

This building has some of the best Norman work to be seen in an English parish church. It was given c1047 by Edward the Confessor to the abbey of Fecamp in Normandy, and by 1086, when William I confirmed the grant, it had become collegiate, hence the scale and elaboration. The church was originally cruciform with a central tower and eastern parts of the early 12th century and an aisled nave of the 1160s or 70s five or six bays long. In the late 16th century everything east of the west arch of the crossing was dismantled and a new chancel built there with chapels on either side, whilst the nave was cut down to four bays and given a large diagonally-buttressed west tower with chequer-work of flint and stone. Despite being of two dates the Norman parts look like a unified design, the changes being in detail rather than layout or proportion. The arcades have tall round piers with multi-scalloped capitals carrying arches of three orders with a profusion of chevrons, and there are large clerestory windows with nook-shafts. Dog-tooth ornament appears on the label of the clerestory on the south side. The surviving arch of the former crossing has a roll-moulding, and others appear on the arch formerly connecting the south transept and aisle, thought to be the earliest part. The capitals on these early 12th century parts have cushion capitals with interlace and lions and below are men grasping tree stems. Of the late medieval period are the large south porch and several windows in the aisles. The chancel east wall and the two bay arcades to the chapels are of 1863 by G.M.Hills, and the tower arch is of 1885. There is a Norman font with a bowl of Sussex marble with chevrons and corner shafts. Original ironwork remains in the south door. In the south aisle are Royal Arms of Queen Anne dated 1703 and the Mace and Staff (of c1685) of the former borough having two M.P.s until 1832.

STOPHAM   *St Mary*   TQ 026190

The late 11th century nave has high but narrow doorways each with a roll-moulding. A blocked early window remains in the chancel. The south doorway has shafts with the capitals composed of three rings. The chancel arch has a roll-moulding and there is another arch in the east wall, suggesting that the three-light 15th century window replaced a Norman apse. This window contains heraldic glass of 1638. The octagonal 15th century font has quatrefoils. Of c1600 are the west tower and the stained glass showing one figure of that period and another in medieval dress of Brian de Stopham, d1273. On the nave floor are brasses of three members of the Barttelot family with their wives, John, d1428, John, d1453, and Richard, d1462. Brasses of a later Richard Barttelot, d1614, and his two wives lie on the chancel floor.

STORRINGTON   *St Mary*   TQ 086141

The original 11th century nave with 13th century openings now forms the north aisle. It has a 13th century arch towards the chancel, opposite which is the original chancel arch re-set. The north arcade is 15th century. A new nave was built in 1750 but the west tower is the principal relic of that campaign, for there was another rebuilding in 1876 when the present south aisle was added.

STOUGHTON   *St Mary*   SU 801115

The nave, narrower chancel and transepts are all late 11th century, although west of the transepts the nave was rebuilt in the 13th century, and the chancel windows and north transept piscina are also of that period. The transepts have double splayed Norman windows but they may not go back to the 11th century, and, since the roll-moulded arches to the transepts are of c1200, the only certain original feature is the chancel arch. This has roll mouldings and triple shafts with capitals of Corinthian type, though crudely executed. In the late 14th century the south transept was converted into a tower with a pyramidal roof, the upper parts being partly supported by a wooden framework inside. There is a 17th century brick south porch. The Norman font is partly re-cut but has scrools arranged like a Tree of Life.

SULLINGTON   *St Mary*   TQ 099131

The nave appears to be Saxon but has no early openings. The chancel has one Norman window on the north side. The arches to the tower and chancel are 13th century but the tower is Norman with a mostly renewed original west doorway. The two bay north arcade is late 13th century but the west arch seems to have orders of different dates and the respond looks earlier. The 14th century east window has reticulated tracery. There is a 15th century font with quatrefoils. The effigy of a 13th century knight in chain-mail is now in a very defaced condition.

SUTTON   *St John*   SU 978156

The 11th century nave has herringbone masonry on the north side. The late 12th century south aisle has an arcade of two full bays with a slight chamfer and waterleaf capitals, plus a narrow plain east arch. The narrow west arch is a Victorian copy of this. The west tower and the chancel are early 14th century, the latter having renewed windows with cusped quatrefoils over two lights, whilst the three-light east window has a circle made up of quatrefoils. There are also a piscina and sedilia with fine mouldings. A shallow north transept of this period was later heightened. The north aisle has one good 15th century window of three lights.

TANGMERE   *St Andrew*   SU 902062

The bell-turret is carried on a timber frame inside the west end of the Norman nave with two original windows on each side and an original plain tub font. One of these windows has a worn carving, possibly re-used Saxon work showing a beheading. The chancel arch and chancel with two wide east lancets are 13th century.

TERWICK   *St Peter*   SU 818234

The nave and chancel are 12th century, but the only unrestored feature of that period is the font. The windows are a mixture of 13th and 19th century lancets and larger 15th century openings. The altar rail is 17th century.

THAKEHAM   *St Mary*   TQ 110174

One Norman window remains on the north side. The north transept has a window set in the arch of a former east chapel. It and the chancel with a piscina and three east lancets under a shafted rere-arch are early 13th century. The forms of the transept arch and piscina show that the south transept was not built until c1300. Of c1500 are the timber south porch and the west tower, plus the octagonal font with a coved stem and panelled base. Monuments to the Apsley family include small brasses to people who died in 1514 and 1515, a life-sized incised slab to John, d1527, tombs of William, d1582, and John, d1587, and a tablet to Edward, d1654.

TILLINGTON   *All Hallows*   SU 964220

The south transeptal tower of 1807 with a Scots-Crown type spire was intended to be a landmark visible from Petworth. Arches inside suggest that it replaced a more modest 13th century tower. The exterior of the church is mostly later 19th century with tiled dormer windows, but the interior has three bay arcades of c1200 with two slightly chamfered orders and crocketed capitals, and there is a 13th century chancel arch. There is a tablet to William Mitford, d1777.

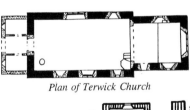

Plan of Terwick Church

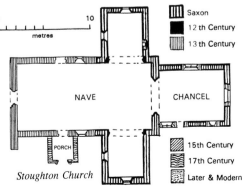

0 ———— 10
metres

	Saxon
	12th Century
	13th Century
	15th Century
	17th Century
	Later & Modern

NAVE   CHANCEL

PORCH

Stoughton Church

Tower at Tillington

TORTINGTON   *St Thomas*   TQ 003049

This church, now maintained by the Churches Conservation Trust, is hidden behind a farm. The nave and chancel of c1140 are connected by a fine arch of two orders, the outermost having beakheads, which are otherwise only found in Sussex at New Shoreham. The south doorway with shafts and two orders of chevrons has presumably been moved twice, once when the two bay south aisle was added in the 13th century, and again c1860 when the long abandoned aisle was reinstated and the arcade opened up again. The chancel has a 13th century lancet in each wall. The nave has original north windows, although renewed outside. There is a Norman font with arcading and pendants, and there is a modest Jacobean pulpit.

TREYFORD   *St Mary*   SU 824187

Hidden amongst trees above the road are ruins of a 13th century single-chamber church abandoned after a new church of St Peter was built to the NW. This in turn was dismantled (blown up) in 1951 and more remains of the older building. The chancel has a piscina and two south lancets and three east lancets. The nave retains a west lancet and one on the north although most of the north wall is missing, whilst the existing south wall is 19th century,, possibly on the site of a former arcade.

Brass at Trotton

TROTTON   *St George*   SU 836225

This is a wide single chamber of four bays with regular buttressing, two-light windows plus a low-side window with a wooden shutter, and two original south doorways plus a blocked doorway on the north. There is an original roof with tie-beams and arched braces rising to collars, with wind-braces on the sides. The oblong west tower may be slightly earlier. Probably of c1380 is a wall-painting of the Last Judgement on the nave west wall. The east window is Victorian. Trotton has two of Britain's best brasses. That of Lady Margaret Camoys, d1310, is the earliest known memorial of this type to a female. She presumably was involved in the building of the church. There are indents in the figure for nine shields and an indent for a surrounding canopy. A full double canopy still survives over the figures of Thomas, Lord Camoys, d1419, and his wife on a tomb chest. The couple hold hands instead of being in prayer as usual. There is another 15th century tomb chest in the nave and in the corners of the chancel are tomb chests of Sir Roger Lewknor, c1478, and Anthony Forster, d1643. The altar rail of unusual type is 17th century.

TWINEHAM   *St Peter*   TQ 253200

This is a small 16th century church with brick used not only for the walls but the windows also. It has a nave and narrower chancel and a diagonally-buttressed west tower. There is a timber south porch and a 19th century organ chamber on the north. The reredos contains Flemish or French panels with Flamboyant tracery of about the same period as the church. The pulpit and the panels in the family pew are Jacobean. Very unusually, part of the churchyard was used by Quakers from 1694 until 1732.

Upper Beeding Church

Tortington Church

UP MARDEN *St Michael* SU 795141

This is a remote, unrestored and little-used church, alone except for a farm. The interior has cream plaster, uneven brick floors, plaster wagon roofs and candelabra, all a joy to behold. The nave and chancel are both 13th century with three lancets on each side in the nave and two on each side in the chancel, whilst the east wall has a stepped group of three. The nave has original doorways to the north, south and west, the latter now opening into a slightly later tower with a weatherboarded bell-chamber which fails to reach the height of the nave roof. The Saxon-looking triangular chancel arch is 16th century and the original arch can be seen above it.

UPPER BEEDING *St Peter* TQ 193111

Originally the chancel was used by the Benedictine priory of Sele nearby to the north, founded by William de Braose in 1075. The existing mid-16th century chancel has a window formed from some late 13th century arcading from the priory, and there is also a re-set doorway. The wide nave has renewed lancets on the north, with foliage on the spandrel between a pair towards the east. The west tower is of c1300. The church was much altered in the 19th century and the south aisle and probably the chancel arch date from then.

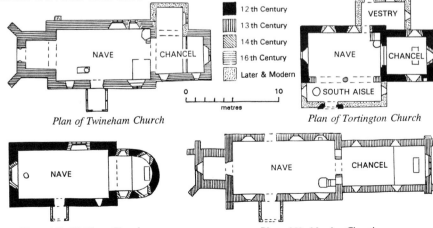

12 th Century
13 th Century
14 th Century
16 th Century
Later & Modern

0   10
metres

VESTRY
NAVE   CHANCEL
SOUTH AISLE

Plan of Twineham Church

Plan of Tortington Church

NAVE

NAVE   CHANCEL

Plan of Up Waltham Church

Plan of Up Marden Church

UP WALTHAM   *St Mary*   SU 795142

This is a small 12th century church of nave and apse, features of that period being the plain south doorway, one south window and the piscina formed by hollowing out the top of a volute capital. The west window and three single lights in the apse are 14th century and the chancel arch is either of then or a little earlier. The church has a full set of chandeliers. There is as bellcote at the west end.

WALBERTON   *St Mary*   SU 972058

Saxon evidence remained in the nave west wall until the sweeping restoration of 1903 by Richard Creed. In the 12th century aisles were added in a piecemeal fashion with various arches of differing widths and heights pierced through the nave walls. The chancel with lancets is 13th century, and there is a north porch of that period also with lancets. Modern timber framing supports the bell-turret with a broach-spire.

WARMINGHURST   *Holy Sepulchre*   TQ 117169

This is a long 13th century single chamber with restored lancets on each side, a roundel facing west, an a three light east window of c1300 with the tracery featuring quatrefoils in circles. The church remained unrestored until 1959, and the only additions are a vestry on the north and a brick porch with east and west entrances (now blocked) on the south. In c1700 a screen was inserted with a tympanum and Royal Arms of Queen Anne over three arched openings of equal width. The altar rails are late 17th century and the font, box pews and three-decker pulpit are 18th century. There are small brasses of Edward Shelley, d1554, and his wife and good quality tablets to John Riches, d1718, and Elizabeth Benet, d1727

WARNHAM   *St Margaret*   TQ 159338

The north aisle and its arcade are late 14th century, and the south transeptal tower is early 16th century. Money towards building the chapel east of the tower was left in 1524. However, the exterior is mostly the work of A.W.Blomfield in 1885. The late 12th century font has arcading on the square bowl. There is a monument with kneeling figures of Sir John Caryll, d1613.

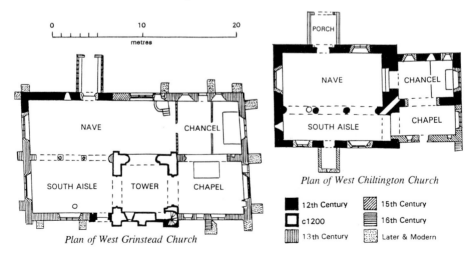

Plan of West Grinstead Church

Plan of West Chiltington Church

■ 12th Century   ▨ 15th Century
□ c1200   ▤ 16th Century
▥ 13th Century   ▦ Later & Modern

West Dean Church

Walberton Church

WASHINGTON   *St Mary*   TQ 119129

The only parts to survive a rebuilding of 1867 by Gordon Hills were the west tower of c1500 and the north arcade with arches and responds of c1200, but the piers and abaci remodelled later in the 13th century.

WESTBOURNE   *St John the Baptist*

Flanking the renewed late 14th century east window are blocked lancets and 13th century walling also survives in the aisles. The piscina, the north vestry, several windows in the aisles, and the west bays engaging the tower are late 14th century but the tower itself and the three bay arcades are early 16th century. The late 14th century windows have two lights splitting into four below the segmental head and there are long hood-moulds. The south porch and SE organ chamber are of the restoration of the 1865 supervised by the vicar, the Reverend John Hanson. There are poorly executed tablets to Henry Barwell, d1785 and Richard Barwell, d1804.

WEST CHILTINGTON   *St Mary*   TQ 090184

The nave has a much restored Norman north doorway with shafts, chevrons and a roll-moulding, and the chancel has one Norman north window. A south aisle added in the late 12th century has an original west window and a three bay arcade of pointed arches on round piers with scallop capitals. The aisle has a long squint into the chancel and a 14th century south doorway with later windows on each side of it. The narrow chancel arch pierces a wall twice as thick as usual to support a shingled central bell-turret with a broach-spire. One of the turret timbers is dated 1602. The chancel has a 13th century triple lancet at the east end and a single arch to a south chapel of that period. There are 12th century wall paintings showing the Majesty and angels with apostles over the west arch of the arcade and further east on both side of the nave are 13th century scenes of the Passion and the life of the Virgin. The north window has a figure of Christ. The pulpit has 16th century linenfold panels with Jacobean decoration above them.

West Grinstead Church

Westhampnett Church

WEST DEAN   *St Andrew*

The Saxon nave has an original tall, narrow north doorway, now blocked. The segmental-headed windows were inserted when the west tower was added in 1727. There had once been a central tower and the church has a crossing, although its arches and the north transept and chancel are mostly of the period after a fire in 1934. The south transept has some late 18th century work and the chancel retains a 13th century east wall with angle-buttresses and three lancets. There are kneeling effigies of Sir Richard Lewknor, d1616, and one of his sons.

WEST GRINSTEAD   *St George*   TQ 171208

The church is rendered and heavily buttressed. The 11th century nave has herringbone masonry on the north with two small windows, one now blocked. The large south transeptal tower was begun c1200. It has a shingled broach-spire sitting on a pyramidal stone roof. About fifty years later the aisle was added or widened and the south chapel added, necessitating new arches to these parts from the tower, while the chancel is even slightly later, having three trefoiled east lancets under a rere-arch. The cinquefoil-headed triple lancets of the nave and aisle west walls must be of c1300. Of the 15th century are one north window and a fine timber porch plus traces of a wall painting of St Christopher between the two, whilst the chancel piscina and the arch beside to the chapel are 16th century. There are brasses with figures of Phillipa de Strabolgi, d1395, and Sir Hugh Halsham, d1441, and his wife, under canopies. There are figures of William Powlett, d1746, and wife in Roman dress, and monuments to Sir Merrik Burrell, d1787, and Sir William Burrell, d1796.

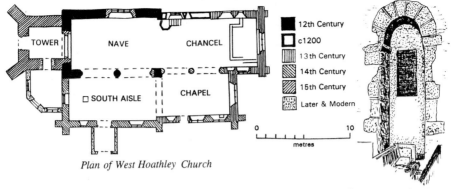

■	12th Century
□	c1200
▥	13th Century
▨	14th Century
▧	15th Century
▦	Later & Modern

Plan of West Hoathley Church

Doorway at West Dean

WESTHAMPNETT   *St Peter*   SU 881061

The east corners of the nave and the west half of the chancel have Saxon masonry. Otherwise the chancel is 13th century with the usual lancets. Parts of the south arcade and the small south transeptal tower with low clasping corner buttresses and a broach-spire are of c1200. In 1867 the south aisle was rebuilt with a new porch in front and a north aisle added with a vestry beyond the north doorway. This doorway is 16th century work re-set with heraldry on the label probably referring to a marriage between the Tawke and Ryman families. The aisle west window is also older work re-set. There are kneeling figures of Richard Sackville and his wife of c1535 set on either side of a defaced Trinity.

WEST HOATHLY   *St Margaret*   TQ 364326

The nave and the west part of the chancel are Norman. An early 13th century south aisle with a two bay arcade of double-chamfered arches and a short round pier was rebuilt wider in the early 14th century. The chancel and south chapel both have restored mid 13th century east windows of three stepped and cusped lancets under one arch with shafting inside, and also of that period are the chancel sedilia and piscina and the north windows with original red painted leaf trails in the embrasures. The two bay south chapel arcade is early 14th century. There is a square 13th century font on five supports. The monuments include a cast iron slab of 1619 with a rim inscription, another of 1624 with the inscription across it, and a plain third one of 1635 with a brass inscription mounted upon it.

WEST ITCHENOR   *St Nicholas*   SU 799006

The 13th century single chamber has three east lancets, several other lancets, an original south doorway and a contemporary octagonal font with arcading. Two windows are 15th century and another is 16th century. The shingled bell-turret is supported on 19th century buttresses. The porch is also 19th century.

WEST STOKE   *St Andrew*   SU 826088

The north doorway now leading to a vestry shows that the nave is 11th century. Of the 13th century are the chancel with lancets on each side and a renewed trefoil-headed piscina and the low porch-tower on the south side of the nave. There are kneeling effigies of Adam Stoughton and his family erected in 1635.

WEST TARRING   *St Andrew*   TQ 131041

The nave and aisles with five bay arcades of double-chamfered arches on circular piers are 13th century, with lancets in both aisles and clerestory. The chancel probably of the 1390s has a five-light east window and two-light side windows. The west tower may also be of that period. There are six stalls with misericords carved with foliage (and one has a head) in the chancel. The knobby altar rail is Jacobean.

WEST THORNEY   *St Nicholas*   SU 769025

This is quite a long church, now lacking both its aisles, although traces of the four bay arcades remain. They were 13th century, and so are the west tower and most of the chancel, with the usual lancets, including three in the east wall and coupled ones in the tower bell-stage, but small Norman window remain on either side of the west part of the chancel. There is an old roof with tie-beams and king-posts. In the north wall is a reset doorway with dogtooth on the label. The tub shaped font with arcading and chevrons is Norman. Part of the screen is 14th century.

WEST WITTERING   *St Peter and St Paul*   SZ 776984

The nave has Norman herringbone masonry. The south arcade of four bays of plain pointed arches on round piers is of c1200. The south chapel can hardly be much later since it has a two bay arcade with round arches towards the chancel. The chancel and the north transeptal tower are 13th century with lancets and clasping corner buttresses. The two east lancets have been renewed in the drastic restoration of 1875 by William White. The chancel has two stalls with misericords, a 17th century altar rail and tombs of William Earnley, d1545, his first wife, d1538. Both have kneeling figures beside central scenes of the Resurrection on one tomb and Christ showing his wounds on the other. There is a 13th century coffin lid in the chapel with a cross and a bishop's pastoral staff.

WIGGONHOLT   *Dedication Unknown*   TQ 060168

The walling of the single chamber may be 12th or 13th century but the windows are mostly late medieval. There is a shingled bell-turret.

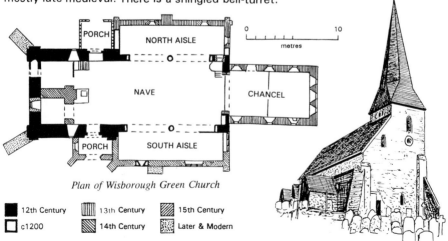

Plan of Wisborough Green Church

Wisborough Green Church

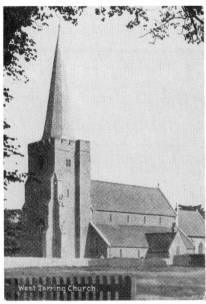

West Tarring Church

Tomb at Wiston Church

WISBOROUGH GREEN   *St Peter ad Vincula*   TQ 052259

The western part of the nave forms a square with massive walls with herringbone masonry of c1100, round headed windows and two plain doorways. One is tempted to suggest that this part was originally intended as huge tower, but if so the two doorways opposite each other must surely be later insertions. Aisles were added to the more thinly walled eastern part of the nave c1200. They are of two wide bays, the south arcade having plain pointed arches on a round pier. The north arcade was replaced c1300 and a clerestory then added. A new chancel was added in the 13th century with three single lancets on each side, a piscina, a north doorway, and three east lancets. In the 14th century the south aisle was rebuilt and a small but lofty tower with a broach-spire was inserted into the nave SW corner. This leaves room for an organ north of it, over which rises the timber stair up to the bell-chamber. The timber north porch and the stone south porch are 15th century. Two old benches with poppy-heads remain in the north porch. A niche to the south of the chancel arch formed a reredos for an altar and has wall-paintings of c1275 with Christ and St James shown above a Crucifixion.

WISTON   *St Mary*   TQ 155124

The church lies beside Wiston Park, far from any village. Restoration in 1862 by G.M.Mills has removed most of the architectural features of interest from what seem to be a 14th century aisle, tower, and chancel added to a 13th century nave probably on 11th century foundations. The tower screen is dated 1635, and there are early 14th century stained glass shields in the east window. The monuments include a brass to Sir John de Brewys, d1426, small figures of Sir Richard Shirley, d1540, standing between his wives, kneeling figures from a monument to Sir Thomas Shirley, d1612, and a monument with a mourning woman to Sarah Goring, d1798.

Saxon nave at Woolbeding

Doorway at Wivelsfield

Effigy at Wiston Church

WIVELSFIELD   *St Peter and St Paul*   TQ 338208

Reset in the north aisle of 1869 by Slater and Carpenter is an 11th century doorway with an arch of two moulded orders. The south arcade of two bays with double-chamfered arches and a short round pier is early 13th century and the chancel with three stepped east lancets and the south chapel are late 13th century. The chapel has an east reredos recess and just one east lancet. Later in the medieval period the nave was lengthened and a SW tower added, high up on which are tiny windows probably created from 11th century material. The base of the pulpit was originally a tester.

Old Print of Worth Church

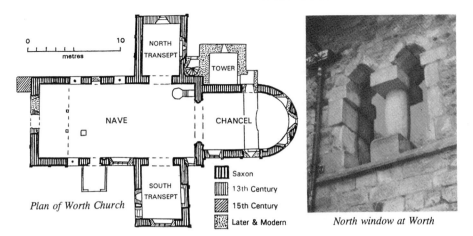

Plan of Worth Church

Saxon
13th Century
15th Century
Later & Modern

North window at Worth

WOODMANCOTE   *Dedication Unknown*   SU 775076

The church was almost entirely rebuilt in 1868 by Woodyer and the only ancient features are a piscina and the king-posts of the nave roof.

WOOLBEDING   *All Hallows*   SU 874227

The Saxon nave has thin pilaster strips on both the north and south sides but no other medieval features remain. The west tower is of 1728, and the nave windows may be of that date, whilst the chancel is of 1870. Two windows contain foreign 16th century glass from Mottisfont Priory in Hampshire. The 18th century reredos now lies on the chancel south wall. There are monuments inside to Dame Margaret Mill, d1744, and the Reverend Sir Henry Mill, d1782, and one outside to Captain John Dodsworth, d1773,

WORTH   *St Nicholas*   TQ 302362

This is an important, almost complete Late Saxon church probably of the early 11th century. It comprises a wide nave, a lower and narrower apsed chancel and two transepts. There are several later medieval windows and a south porch of 1886, plus a tower with a broach-spire added north of the chancel by Salvin during his drastic restoration of 1871. An old print suggests that there was a north tower and spire beforehand (possibly a conversion of the transept), and shows that the nave roof was then of lower pitch and consequently not as high as that of the apsed chancel. The latter was then heavily buttressed and had to be almost entirely rebuilt to return it to its early medieval form. All the parts of the Saxon church have thin pilaster strips carrying a horizontal band. Above this the nave retains three original two-light windows with mid-wall shafts, openings such as this being familiar in Saxon towers but not found anywhere else in a nave. Parts of the tall and narrow nave doorway also remain. There are original arches surviving from the nave into both transepts and the chancel, the latter with semi-circular responds and cushion capitals.

The square font has tracery patterns of c1300. The pulpit with angle columns and Christ and the four evangelists in niched panels is dated 1577 with a German inscription. The altar rail is also a foreign import and seems to have work of c1600 and c1700. The panelling in the south transept is Jacobean. There are late 17th century chandeliers. None of the monuments are early or of importance.

Arcade at Yapton

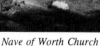

Nave of Worth Church

South side of Yapton Church

YAPTON *St Mary*   SU 982035

The narrow aisles with arcades of pointed single-chamfered arches on octagonal piers are of c1180-1200 and with them goes the SW tower with two-light bell-openings under outer pointed arches. The tower has developed a lean and is now heavily buttressed. This and the 17th century dormer windows add much to the rustic charm of the church. The roofs come almost down to the ground and the very low south aisle outer wall has two round openings close to ground level. The 13th century chancel has lancet windows and a double-chamfered chancel arch on fluted corbels. An east window of 1902 replaces an 18th century window. The timber-framed west porch is late medieval. The Norman font is a tub with relief arcading enclosing Maltese crosses and a and of chevrons round the rim. The best of the tablets are those of John Edmonds, d1687, and Stephen Roe, d1766.

OTHER ANGLICAN CHURCHES IN WEST SUSSEX

ALDWICK - St Richard - 1933 by F.G.Troup. Of little interest.
BOGNOR REGIS - St John Baptist - 1882 by A.W.Blomfield. Polycrome brick inside.
BOGNOR REGIS - St John Baptist - Tower only of Daniel Wonham's church of 1821.
BOGNOR REGIS - St Wilfred - 1908 by G.H.Fellowes Prynne. Never completed.
BURGESS HILL - St John 1861-3 by T.Talbot Bury. SW tower. Black & yellow brick.
BURGESS HILL - St Andrew - 1907-9 by Lacy W Ridge. Wide, with transepts. Brick.
CHICHESTER - All Saints - 1869 probably by Woodyer. Apsed.
CHICHESTER - St George - 1901 by Cutts & Cutts. Nine aisled bays without break.
CHICHESTER - St John - 1812-3 by James Elmes. Elongated white brick octagon.
CHICHESTER - St Paul - 1836 by J.Butler.
COPTHORNE - St John Evangelist - 1877, Habershon & Brock. Rock-faced. NW tower
CRAWLEY - St Peter - 1892-3 by W.Hilton Nash. At West Green.
CRAWLEY: new churches: St Richard 1954, St Mary 1958, St Alban 1961.
DUNCTON - Holy Trinity - 1866. South tower. Decorated style.
EBERNOE - Holy Trinity - 1867 by Habershon & Brock.
HIGHBROOK - All Saints - 1884 by Carpenter & Ingelow.
HORSHAM - St Mark - 1840, but mostly of 1870 by Habershon & Brock.
HUNSTON - St Ledger - Rebuilt in 1885 by A.W.Blomfield.
IPING - Tower 1840, rest 1886 by Loftus Brock. Contains 18th century tablet.
LITTLEHAMPTON - St Mary - 1826, G.Draper, much rebuilt 1934, Randoll Blacking.
LOWFIELD HEATH - St Michael - 1867 by Burges. SW tower with spire.
MIDDLETON - St Nicholas - 1849 by John Elliot. Original church destroyed by sea.
NORTH CHAPEL - 1877 by Salvin except for tower c1820. Font dated 1662.
PARTRIDGE GREEN - St Michael - 1890. Flint outside, brick inside.
PLAISTOW - Holy Trinity - 1851 by J.Butler. Replaced a half-timbered church.
ROFFEY - All Saints - 1878 by A.W.Blomfield. Large SE tower.
SENNICOTTS - St Mary - 1829 perhaps by Draper. Single chamber and west tower.
STANSTED - Christchurch - 1856, possibly by Teulon. Grouped with a school.
SOUTHBOURNE - St John - 1876 by T. Chatfield Clark.
SOUTHWATER - Holy Innocents - 1850 by J.P.Harrison.
STAPLEFIELD - St Mark - 1847 by Benjamin Ferrey. Three tier bellcote. Lancets.
WARNINGLID - St Andrew - 1935 by F.G.Troup. Brick. Round-headed lancets.
WEST LAVINGTON - St Mary Magdalen - 1850 by William Butterfield.
WORTHING - Christ Church - 1841 by John Elliott. Typical "Commissioners' Gothic".
WORTHING - Holy Trinity - 1882 by Coe & Robinson. Altered 17th century pulpit.
WORTHING - St George - 1868 by George Truefitt. Single chamber with apse.
WORTHING - St Paul - 1812 by J.B.Rebecca. Classical. Chancel and roof of 1893.

OTHER CHAPELS IN SUSSEX

BAILIFFSCOURT - late 13th century, lancets & three light east window.
BILSHAM - 13th century chapel used as shed at farm.
OLD ERRINGHAM - 13th century chancel with lancets now used as a barn.
OTTEHAM COURT - Good 14th century chapel at former monastic grange.

FURTHER READING

Sussex, Buildings of England series, Ian Nairn & Nikolaus Pevsner, 1965
Victoria County History of Sussex, several volumes, various dates
Sussex Archeological Collections (published annually)
The Parish Churches of Sussex, John C.Allen, 1984
Ancient Churches of Sussex, Ken & Joyce Whiteman, 1988
Saxon Churches of Sussex, E.A.Fisher, 1986
Exploring Sussex Churches, John E.Vigar

MAP OF CHURCHES IN EAST SUSSEX

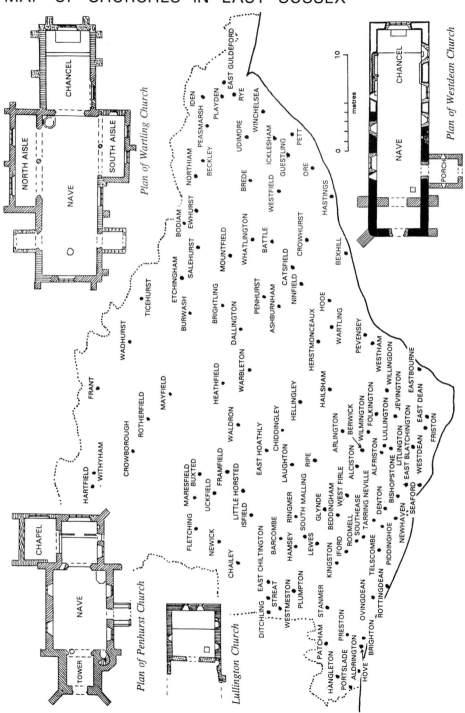

Plan of Wartling Church

Plan of Westdean Church

Plan of Penhurst Church

Lullington Church

CHANCEL

NORTH AISLE

NAVE

SOUTH AISLE

CHANCEL

NAVE

PORCH

CHAPEL

NAVE

TOWER

10

metres

5

0

EAST GULDEFORD
RYE
IDEN
PLAYDEN
WINCHELSEA
PEASMARSH
UDIMORE
NORTHIAM
BECKLEY
ICKLESHAM
WESTFIELD
GUESTLING
PETT
BREDE
ORE
HASTINGS
BODIAM
EWHURST
ETCHINGHAM
MOUNTFIELD
WHATLINGTON
SALEHURST
BATTLE
CROWHURST
BURWASH
BRIGHTLING
CATSFIELD
TICEHURST
PENHURST
NINFIELD
BEXHILL
DALLINGTON
ASHBURNHAM
WADHURST
HOOE
HERSTMONCEAUX
WARBLETON
WARTLING
MAYFIELD
HEATHFIELD
PEVENSEY
FRANT
WESTHAM
ROTHERFIELD
WALDRON
WILLINGDON
WITHAM
WILLINGTON
HELLINGLEY
HAILSHAM
WESTHAM
CROWBOROUGH
FRAMFIELD
HARTFIELD
MARESFIELD
EAST HOATHLY
WILMINGTON
EASTBOURNE
BUXTED
CHIDDINGLEY
BERWICK
JEVINGTON
FLETCHING
LITTLE HORSTED
ARLINGTON
FOLKINGTON
EAST DEAN
UCKFIELD
LAUGHTON
LULLINGTON
FRISTON
ISFIELD
RIPE
ALCISTON
EAST BLATCHINGTON
NEWICK
ALFRISTON
WESTDEAN
BARCOMBE
WEST FIRLE
LITLINGTON
CHAILEY
BEDDINGHAM
BISHOPSTONE
EAST CHILTINGTON
HAMSEY
SOUTH MALLING
TARRING NEVILLE
DITCHLING
RINGMER
DENTON
SEAFORD
STREAT
GLYNDE
IFORD
SOUTHEASE
WESTMESTON
LEWES
RODMELL
NEWHAVEN
PLUMPTON
KINGSTON
PIDDINGHOE
STANMER
TELSCOMBE
PATCHAM
ROTTINGDEAN
PRESTON
OVINGDEAN
HANGLETON
PORTSLADE
BRIGHTON
ALDRINGTON
HOVE

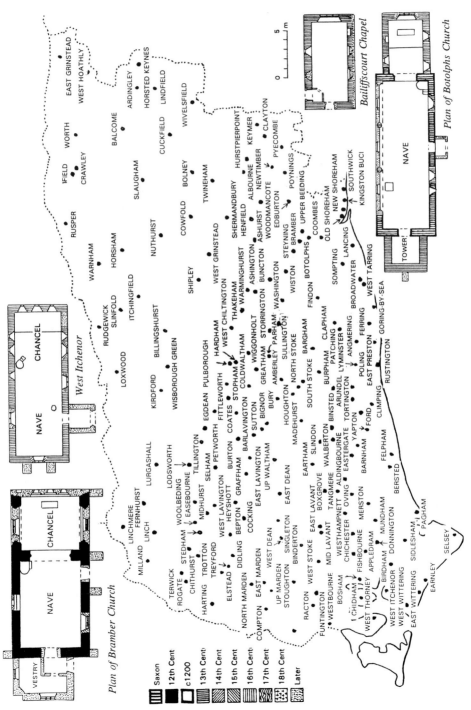

MAP OF CHURCHES IN WEST SUSSEX

Bailiffscourt Chapel

Plan of Botolphs Church

NAVE

TOWER

West Itchenor

CHANCEL

NAVE

Plan of Bramber Church

CHANCEL

NAVE

VESTRY

EAST GRINSTEAD
WEST HOATHLY
ARDINGLEY
HORSTED KEYNES
LINDFIELD
WEST KEYNES
WIVELSFIELD
BALCOME
CUCKFIELD
WORTH
IFIELD
CRAWLEY
RUSPER
SLAUGHAM
BOLNEY
COWFOLD
TWINEHAM
HURSTPIERPOINT
KEYMER
CLAYTON
NEWTIMBER
PYECOMBE
ALBOURNE
WOODMANCOTE
SHERMANDBURY
HENFIELD
ASHURST
POYNINGS
EDBURTON
UPPER BEEDING
STEYNING
BRAMBER
COOMBES
WARNHAM
HORSHAM
NUTHURST
WEST GRINSTEAD
SHIPLEY
WARMINGHURST
THAKEHAM
WEST CHILTINGTON
STORRINGTON
BUNCTON
WASHINGTON
WISTON
FINDON
BOTOLPHS
OLD SHOREHAM
NEW SHOREHAM
SOUTHWICK
KINGSTON BUCI
SOMPTING
LANCING
BROADWATER
WEST TARRING
GORING-BY-SEA
RUDGEWICK
SLINFOLD
ITCHINGFIELD
BILLINGSHURST
WISBOROUGH GREEN
LOXWOOD
KIRDFORD
EGDEAN
PULBOROUGH
HARDHAM
COLDWALTHAM
STOPHAM
WIGGONHOLT
GREATHAM
AMBERLEY
PARHAM
SULLINGTON
NORTH STOKE
SOUTH STOKE
BARGHAM
CLAPHAM
PATCHING
ANGMERING
FERRING
EAST PRESTON
RUSTINGTON
CLIMPING
PETWORTH
FITTLEWORTH
COATES
BARLAVINGTON
SUTTON
BIGNOR
BURY
HOUGHTON
MADEHURST
BURPHAM
ARUNDEL
LYMINSTER
POLING
FORD
LURGASHALL
LODSWORTH
TILLINGTON
SELHAM
BURTON
GRAFFHAM
EAST LAVINGTON
UP WALTHAM
EAST DEAN
SLINDON
WALBERTON
BINSTED
EASTERGATE
TORTINGTON
YAPTON
BARNHAM
FELPHAM
BERSTED
LINCHMERE
FERNHURST
LINCH
MILLAND
TERWICK
ROGATE
STEDHAM
CHITHURST
TROTTON
TREYFORD
ELSTEAD
WEST LAVINGTON
HEYSHOTT
DIDLING
BEPTON
COCKING
WEST DEAN
SINGLETON
BINDERTON
EAST MARDEN
WEST STOKE
MID LAVANT
EAST LAVANT
TANGMERE
ALDINGBOURNE
OVING
MERSTON
MUNDHAM
DONNINGTON
SIDLESHAM
PAGHAM
EARNLEY
SELSEY
HARTING
NORTH MARDEN
COMPTON
UP MARDEN
STOUGHTON
RACTON
FUNTINGTON
WESTBOURNE
WESTHAMPNETT
CHICHESTER
BOSHAM
CHIDHAM
WEST THORNEY
WEST ITCHENOR
WEST WITTERING
EAST WITTERING
FISHBOURNE
APPLEDRAM
BIRDHAM
BOXGROVE
EARTHAM
MIDHURST
EASEBOURNE
WOOLBEDING

Legend

Saxon
12th Cent
c1200
13th Cent
14th Cent
15th Cent
16th Cent
17th Cent
18th Cent
Later

0   5 m

GLOSSARY OF ARCHITECTURAL TERMS

Abacus	- A flat slab on top of a capital.
Apse	- Semi-circular or polygonal east end of a church containing an altar.
Ashlar	- Masonry of blocks with even faces and square edges.
Baroque	- A whimsical and odd form of the Classical architectural style.
Beakhead	- Decorative motif of bird or beast heads, often biting a roll moulding.
Broaches	- Sloping half pyramids adapting an octagonal spire to a square tower.
Cartouche	- A tablet with an ornate frame, usually enclosing an inscription.
Chancel	- The eastern part of a church used by the clergy.
Chevron Ornament	- A Norman ornament with continuous Vs forming a zig-zag.
Clerestory	- An upper storey pierced by windows lighting the floor below.
Collar Beam	- A tie-beam used higher up near the apex of the roof.
Corbel Table	- A row of corbels supporting the eaves of a roof.
Crossing Tower	- A tower built on four arches in the middle of a cruciform church.
Cruciform Church	- A cross-shaped church with transepts forming the arms of the cross.
Cusp	- A projecting point between the foils of a foiled Gothic arch.
Dado	- The decorative covering of the lower part of a wall or screen.
Decorated	- The architecture style in vogue in England c1300-1380.
Dog Tooth	- Four-cornered stars placed diagonally and raised pyramidally.
Easter Sepulchre	- A recess in a chancel which received an effigy of Christ at Easter.
Elizabethan	- Of the time of Queen Elizabeth I (1558-1603).
Fan Vault	- Vault with fan-like patterns. In fashion from c1440 to 1530.
Foil	- A lobe formed by the cusping of a circle or arch.
Four Centred Arch	- A low, flattish arch with each curve drawn from two compass points.
Gargoyle	- A water spout shaped like an animal or human head below a parapet.
Green Man	- A figure with foliage or fruit coming from the mouth and-or hair, etc.
Head Stops	- Heads of humans or beasts forming the ends of a hoodmould.
Herringbone Masonry	- Courses of stones alternately sloping at 45 degrees to horizontal.
Hoodmould	- A projecting moulding above a lintel or arch to throw off water.
Jacobean	- Of the time of King James I (1603-25).
Jamb	- The side of a doorway, window, or other opening.
King-post	- A post connecting a tie-beam or collar-beam with the roof ridge beam.
Lancet	- A long and comparatively narrow window with a pointed head.
Light	- A compartment of a window.
Lintel	- A horizontal stone or beam spanning an opening.
Merlon	- An upstanding part of a crenellated parapet. The indents are crenels.
Miserichord	- Bracket underneath hinged choir stall seat to support standing person.
Mullion	- A vertical member dividing the lights of a window.
Nave	- The part of a church in which the congregation sits or stands.
Norman	- A division of English Romanesque architecture from 1066 to 1200.
Ogival Arch	- Arch of oriental origin with both convex and concave curves.
Pediment	- Low-pitched gable used in classical and neo-classical architecture.
Perpendicular	- The architectural style in vogue in England c1380-1540.
Pilaster	- Flat buttress or pier attached to a wall.
Piscina	- A stone basin used for rinsing out holy vessels after a mass.
Plinth	- The projecting base of a wall.
Queen-posts	- Two vertical struts placed symmetrically on a tie-beam or collar-beam.
Quoins	- Dressed stones at the corners of a building.
Rere-Arch	- An arch on the inside face of a window embrasure or doorway.
Reredos	- Structure behind and above an altar forming a backdrop to it.
Respond	- A half pier or column bonded into a wall and carrying an arch.
Reticulation	- Tracery with a net-like appearence. Current c1330-70.
Rood Screen	- A screen with a crucifix mounted on it between a nave and chancel.
Sedilia	- Seats for clergy (usually three) in the south wall of a chancel.
Spandrel	- The surface between two arches or between an arch and a corner.
Squint	- Opening allowing the main altar to be seen from a subsiderary one.
Tester	- A sounding board above a 17th or 18th century pulpit.
Tie-Beam	- A beam connecting the slopes of a roof at or near its foot.
Tracery	- Intersecting ribwork in the upper part of a later Gothic window.
Transom	- A horizontal member dividing the lights of a window.
Tympanum	- The space between the lintel of a doorway and the arch above it.
Venetian Window	- Window with square headed lights on either side of an arched light.
Victorian	- Of the time of Queen Victoria (1837-1901).
Voussoir	- A wedge shaped stone forming part of an arch.
Wall Plate	- A timber laid longitudinally along the top of a wall.